Skin Deep

SMART TALK

Skin Deep

Susan Wallach

Troll Associates

ACKNOWLEDGEMENT

A special thanks to Dr. Allyn Beth Landau, M.D. for her time and expert assistance in assuring that the information contained in this book is sound and accurate.

Library of Congress Cataloging-in-Publication Data

Wallach, Susan.
  Skin deep / by Susan Wallach; illustrated by Donald Richey.
    p.   cm.—(Smart talk)
  Summary: All about skin—how to care for skin, cosmetics,
environment and skin, applying makeup—and information on hair care
and styling, too.
  ISBN 0-8167-1997-7 (lib. bdg.)   ISBN 0-8167-1998-5 (pbk.)
  1. Skin—Care and hygiene—Juvenile literature. 2. Teenage girls—
Health and hygiene—Juvenile literature. 3. Grooming for girls—
Juvenile literature. [1. Skin—Care and hygiene. 2. Hair—Care
and hygiene. 3. Beauty, Personal.] I. Richey, Donald, ill.
II. Title. III. Series.
RL87.W35   1991
646.7'26—dc20   89-39936

Table of Contents

What's It All About?

Congratulations! You are in the process of becoming a young woman.

What?

Are you saying so what? Big deal! What's so special about that?

Everything is special about this time. And everything is special about you.

Look around you. Who besides you and your friends has as much going on in her life with all sorts of changes happening inside and out? Who else is balancing on the tightrope of childhood and adulthood? Who else has all these wonderful and new feelings which are changing the way you see yourself and the world?

Who is transforming from a girl into a young woman? You are, that's who!

Sure, lots of other people have been in your shoes (or sneakers), but this is the first time you are here.

You're on an adventure—a quest. A quest to discover who you are, who you are becoming, and how to be the most you can be.

Wait!

Is there still some doubt that any of this has to do with you? Take the following quiz:

✩✩ QUIZ ✩✩

1. *When you walk by a mirror, do you:*
   a. Pretend not to look, sneak a glance at yourself and look away quickly?
   b. Rush right up to it and stare at yourself?
   c. Walk by it as quickly as possible, making sure you don't see yourself?
   d. Stop, calmly see how you look, and then walk on?
   e. All of the above, depending on the day?

2. *Does your body suddenly seem:*
   a. Too big?
   b. Too small?
   c. Unrecognizable?
   d. Just right?
   e. All of the above, depending on the day?

3. *Is your hair:*
   a. The worst mess you've ever seen?
   b. The most unmanageable it's ever been?
   c. The wrong color, texture, cut?
   d. Just perfect?
   e. All of the above, depending on the day?

4. *Is your skin:*
   a. A mass of hideous bumps and pimples?
   b. Too pale?
   c. Too dark?
   d. Smooth, with good color?
   e. All of the above, depending on the day?

5. *Do you feel:*
   a. Like the biggest monster who ever lived?
   b. Like an orphan who everyone hates?
   c. Like someone you don't even recognize?
   d. Like yourself, a person who is fun and interesting?
   e. All of the above, depending on the day?

6. *Do you sometimes wish you could:*
   a. Never grow up?
   b. Be twenty-five already?
   c. Wear outrageous clothing and never have to do anything serious?
   d. Discover the lost city of Atlantis and save the world?
   e. All of the above, depending on the day?

✩✩✩

If you chose any of the answers above, all of the answers above, or some of the answers above — you are exactly normal for where you are right now in your life.

Yes, this confirms it. You are becoming a young woman.

For you, every day, or even every hour, might mean a new emotion. One moment you feel like a child, the next an adult — and the next, who-knows-what. Everything is fine and nothing is fine. Everyone around you might seem so different or so much the same that you could scream.

Your mirror is your best friend one day and your worst enemy the next. Your hair, which you hardly even noticed six months ago, is now your most beautiful asset or the very thing ruining your life.

You are neither a very young girl nor a woman, but somewhere in the middle, and that's the hardest place to be. It's a time for changing and growing, both physically and emotionally. It's as if you are shedding old skin like a snake — the old skin doesn't quite fit, but at least it's familiar and you're not quite sure what the new skin will look or feel like. It's a time of excitement, change and uncertainty.

The one thing to remember is that you are not alone in this. It is this way for everyone — although each person goes through this in her own way and in her own time.

This book is especially for you. SKIN DEEP is designed to answer those questions that maybe you can't quite ask others or don't even know who to ask.

Here's what we have in store for you in SKIN DEEP:

Chapter Two — It's all about skin: how to care for it, how to determine the kind of skin you have, and what to do when your skin breaks out.

Chapter Three — It's all about skin treatment: which products are really good for you, and which ones you should avoid.

Chapter Four — It's all about your skin and your environment: everything from diet to weather, from sleep to exercise, and how it affects your skin. We'll give you plenty of tips to keep it healthy and glowing.

Chapter Five — It's all about beautifying yourself. This chapter will help you figure out if you want to wear makeup or if the natural look is right for you. Either way, we'll guide you through the makeup maze.

Chapter Six — It's all about hair care: from hair type analysis to washing, conditioning, and styling tools.

Chapter Seven — It's all about hair styling. We'll talk about haircuts, the best styles for you, taming your hair with all the great new hair products, experimenting with hair accessories, playing with color, and ending with creating great new looks.

SKIN DEEP also has fun quizzes, charts, do's and don'ts, easy-to-follow drawings, and tons of information.

All of this is waiting for you! Welcome to your new world!

The Skin Scene

Skin! Does it feel like you can't live with it and you can't live without it?

Jennifer remembers when her skin was just skin, and she would wash it when it was dirty. Now, it's something that she has to really take care of.

Lisa feels like she just discovered her skin; she loves the softness of it and how sometimes she feels it glows.

Stefi just doesn't get it. Her skin feels different than it used to. She washes it often and it still feels oily. What's going on? It didn't do this last year!

Skin.

It's transforming before your eyes, and why? Because you're growing up and changes are happening within your body which affect the outside of your body.

Before discussing how to take care of your skin, it would be helpful to understand what is happening to you physically — it's called puberty. Puberty occurs at different times for everyone — but as you're becoming a teenager the balance of hormones in your body starts to change. This one change in your body affects all of you. Here are some of the physical changes you can expect: Your breasts will develop, you'll grow hair on different parts of your body, you'll grow taller, and your sweat and oil glands will either enlarge, creating more oil underneath your skin, or stay small, not sending enough oil to your skin.

So it's part of what naturally happens as you grow older. There are specific things you can do to care for your skin during this time and we will get into that shortly.

YOUR WASHING RITUAL

With the excitement and fun of growing up, there are also the responsibilities. You need to take care of yourself so you feel good about who you are. And the phrase "caring for yourself" is key here — caring for yourself in a physical way is just as important as caring for yourself emotionally. Remember, you deserve to be well taken care of! So start a good washing ritual for yourself now so you can develop healthy, clean habits and avoid skin problems.

Why not try to make caring for yourself — such as washing, cleaning your room, doing your homework — fun and exciting. Taking care of your skin is really showing respect for yourself, so begin with a cleansing ritual that tells the world you want to look your best!

The first thing to know is that your skin is delicate and sensitive — you don't want to do anything to startle it. You don't want your skin to be irritated and get back at you by causing your skin to break out, develop a rash, or turn red or flaky. So, use warm water when washing your face, and be gentle with your skin. There is no need to scrub your face clean no matter what you've heard. Avoid washcloths, loofah sponges, and skin brushes. You don't have to hurt yourself to get clean. In this case — no pain, lots of gain. Be gentle!

The most important ingredient in cleaning your face is water! Your body is made up of mostly water and our environment is made up of mostly water. And water is the healthiest and purest way to clean your skin.

If you're using a special facial cleanser instead of soap, the key ingredient in the cleanser should also be water — the creams, oils, and detergents should be listed later in the ingredients. A water soluble cleanser rinses clean without the need of a washcloth.

The feeling you want after you wash your face is soft and supple. Your face needn't feel tight in order to be clean; nor should it feel greasy. The right kind of soap for you will gently take the dirt off your skin, but will not block your pores or abrade your skin.

Not all soaps are the same and in fact, they are not all called soaps. The following is a list of the different kinds of products that you will find in the stores.

FACE SOAPS
These basically contain animal or vegetable fats and are usually good for people with oily skin, but they can be drying.

MILD SKIN CLEANSERS
These are broken up into different groups and are usually better for girls with dry skin, but some cleansers are better than others.

✪ Superfatted soaps contain extra amounts of fats and oils and can leave a greasy residue on the skin (leaving you with a not quite clean feeling).

✪ Transparent soaps, which are clear, have more fat in them than regular bath soaps. The transparency comes from the glycerin, sugar, and alcohol that are included.

✪ Soapless soaps are synthetically made and don't leave a film of grease on your face.

✪ Washable creams and lotions are basically moisturizing lotions with soaps or synthetic soap added. These are very good for people with very dry skin.

SOAPS WITH SPECIAL ADDITIVES
✪ Herbs, fruits, or vegetables — There is no evidence that these "natural" additions actually do anything for your skin. You could be allergic to them, and it costs money to have these extra ingredients added.

✪ Perfumes and dyes — These ingredients don't add to the soap's ability to clean and they might irritate your skin.

✪ Abrasives — apricot pits, oatmeal, bran, etc. — These soaps can be irritating and harmful to your skin, which is exactly what you don't want.

✪ Medications — These soaps probably don't do as much as they promise, for they are rinsed off before the "medication" can really do much. They also might be irritating to dry or sensitive skin.

DEODORANT SOAPS

These are soaps with certain chemicals added to hold back the production of odor-producing bacteria. Some of them also contain fragrances. You certainly don't need this kind of soap on your face, for your face does not have odor-producing sweat glands.

Before you go out and start buying soaps, check the bathrooms at home. What kind of soap does your mother use? It's probably different than the soap your father uses. Also, there may be a different soap in the shower than at the sink. You do want to be sure that you aren't using a deodorant soap on your face.

You and your mother might have the same skin types, which we'll get into later in this chapter, but you might not. She is also older than you and might need different things for her skin.

The soap in your home might be perfect for you. But if you feel it isn't after you finish reading these chapters on skin, talk with your mother and let her know that you might need a special soap for your skin. She might also be able to help you determine your skin type and pick out the right kind of soap when you go shopping.

When you buy a new type of soap, test it out. See how your skin reacts. It's most important to pay attention to what your skin tells you. If it burns or gets irritated, then stop using that soap. If your skin feels clean and smooth, then it's probably the right soap for you.

You need to wash your face at least twice a day — in the morning and at night. Do not skip this treat for yourself no matter how tired you are or how you feel. Take the time to take care of yourself.

After you have washed your face gently, pat your face dry. Do not rub or pull your skin. Remember, be gentle. Also, be especially careful of the skin around your eyes, for this is the most sensitive area of your face.

CLEANSING RITUAL IN THREE EASY STEPS

Splash Water on Face and Gently Lather *Rinse Thoroughly* *Pat Dry*

YOUR SKIN TYPE

The kind of skin you have is determined by many things, such as the environment, your emotions, your menstrual cycle, and possibly your diet — all of which will be dealt with in Chapter Four. But mainly, your skin type is hereditary. The kind of skin you have has already been determined. So you don't have much control over whether your skin is dry, oily, sensitive, or prone to breakouts. All you can do is care for your skin to make sure it's as healthy and clean as it can be.

You've already heard of normal, oily, dry, and combination skin. Let's put one myth to rest right here — most people don't have normal skin. What is normal? It is some arbitrary designation that someone somewhere has made up. So do not feel abnormal because you do not have normal skin. In fact, you are probably more normal than anyone claiming to have perfect skin. Very few young women have perfect skin!

☆☆   QUIZ   ☆☆

In order to tell what kind of skin you have, take the following test:

1. *Wash your face and then wait an hour.*

2. *Stand in the sunlight with a mirror, and examine your forehead, cheeks, hairline, chin, and nose.*

3. *Ask yourself the following questions:*
   a. Is my skin greasy with open pores?
   b. Is my skin flaky, rough, or red with invisible pores?

c. Are my forehead, nose, and chin greasy? Are
   my cheeks red, possibly flaky?
   d. Are my pores small and does my skin feel and
   look smooth?
4. *Touch your finger to your forehead. Is it greasy or
   dry?*

☆☆☆

If you answered yes to "a", then your skin is more on
the oily side. If you answered yes to "b" you more than
likely have dry skin. A yes answer to "c" means that
you have combination skin. If "d" fit you, then you are
one of those fortunate few (dare we say it?) who
happen to have "normal" skin and just need to main-
tain it.

If your forehead felt greasy, it is another indication
that you probably have oily skin. On the other hand, if
your forehead was rough feeling and perhaps flaky,
then your skin is dry.

That wasn't too hard, was it?

In addition to fitting one of the above categories, you
may also have sensitive skin. Sensitive skin reacts
quickly to anything. You might get heat rashes; you
might get hives from holding an animal; you might
break out from wearing a certain type of makeup; your
skin might show scratches easily or turn red in reaction to a new shampoo. You will know if your skin is
sensitive by observing how it reacts to different situ-
ations and products.

It may be too soon to know what type of skin you
have. And that is fine. Right now, it might seem to fit

into the normal category. It might be that your body hasn't started changing yet, but it's still important to wash your face properly, regularly, and gently.

Before getting into the different skin types, remember that your skin is alive and changes. Right now, you know whether it's "normal," oily, dry, or a combination of the two. Over the years, your skin type might change and then you'll need to change your soap and your washing routine.

OILY SKIN

A lot of girls fall in this category so you are not alone. Oily skin means your oil glands are producing more oil than is necessary. In some cases, the overproduction of oil causes pimples, blackheads and/or whiteheads, which will be dealt with later. Right now, it is important to know how to take care of basic oily skin.

So — you have oily skin. Don't despair. You just need to watch out for a few things. First of all, you want to be sure not to let the oil block up your pores. You want to use a soap or cleanser that has more water than oil, so water should come first in the list of ingredients.

✪ You might choose face soaps or soapless soaps. Again, you can tell best by what is working. You don't want to dry out your skin. Yes, even people with oily skin can dry out their skin by using soaps that are too harsh or soaps that abrade their skin. If you can, try experimenting a little by buying small samples.

✪ Because your glands are producing more oil than they need to, wash your face three times a day.

✪ In between washings, blot the oil off with face blotters that you can buy in the drug store, or soft tissues can work almost as well. Treat your oily skin gently. Don't rub the oil off— your skin will react by producing more oil.

✪ There are also some astringents and toners that can be used carefully and sparingly, but be sure to look for astringents with low or no alcohol content.

✪ Remember being told "don't put money in your mouth for you don't know where it's been?" Your hands have been in more places than your money ever has so you definitely don't want to put these carriers of dirt and bacteria on your face.

You may not even be aware that you are touching your skin. As you read this line, notice where your hands are. Are you leaning on them as you read; are they (oh-no) picking at your skin? When you are in class, on the phone, or studying, are your hands on your face? You will eventually become more aware of what you do with your hands and soon it will become second nature to you to keep them away from your face.

Touching, picking, and rubbing your face irritates your skin. Irritated skin fights back by becoming more oily and breaking out.

Also, when you can, keep your hair off your face, and always make sure your hair is clean. Your hair will not increase the amount of oil produced, but it can add more oil to the surface of your skin and it might increase your chances of breaking out.

You may have heard that chocolate, french fries, soda, potato chips and many other similar types of food are bad for your skin. None of this has been proven either one way or the other. Some experts believe that food doesn't affect your skin at all. Others say your skin reacts only if you're allergic to certain foods. Still others believe that foods high in fat, salt, and spices increase your oil production. Food is definitely a very controversial area and one that will be covered in Chapter Four.

DO's for oily skin

1. Use a soap that contains more water than oil (water-based) and that is gentle to your skin.
2. Wash your face three times a day.
3. Blot off the excess oil gently with face blotters bought in the drug store.
4. Use low- or non-alcohol astringents when you can't wash your face during the day.

DON'Ts for oily skin

1. Don't touch your face unnecessarily.
2. If you are allergic to certain foods, stay away from them.
3. Don't use products that contain oils on your face.

DRY SKIN

Dry skin lacks the proper oil to keep water on the skin. Therefore, your skin flakes, feels dry, and sometimes reddens. Your skin lacks moisture. The good news about dry skin is that you're less likely to break out as frequently as someone with oily skin although you aren't completely free from dreaded break-out attacks.

✪ If you have dry skin, wash your face only twice a day. You will probably need a mild skin cleanser instead of soap, one that contains ingredients that will hold moisture to your skin. Humectants, such as glycerin, lactic acid, and propylene glycol, are ingredients that bind moisture to your skin.

✪ If your skin is *very* dry you might also need a light moisturizer. We will discuss these in detail in the next chapter.

✪ Remember to pay attention to your skin and see what your skin needs. Don't predetermine that your skin is dry and lavish oil all over your face. If you do this, you might find that you have another problem — clogged pores from putting too much oil on your face, which result in pimples.

✪ If your skin is dry, you may also have sensitive skin — skin that can't handle certain types of products. Treat your skin gently and see how the soap and/or moisturizer works on your skin.

✪ If your skin becomes oily, it might be because your soap and/or moisturizer is too oily and is clogging your skin.

✪ At this age, you might not need a moisturizer yet. Stick with a gentle soap or a soap that contains moisturizing ingredients and see how your skin reacts. This may be enough for now.

✪ One final word on dry skin: There is a strong belief that dry skin causes wrinkles; that if you have dry skin, your face will be sagging by age twenty. THIS IS UNTRUE!

Your dry skin is your surface skin. Wrinkles are basically a result of age and sun exposure. So don't panic! You are not doomed to wrinkled skin at an early age.

DO's for dry skin

1. Wash your face twice a day.
2. Use a gentle moisturizer on your skin when necessary.
3. Pay attention to how your skin reacts.

DON'Ts for dry skin

1. Don't use an astringent.
2. Don't pull at your skin.
3. Don't use too much oil on your face.

★★★

COMBINATION SKIN

Combination skin is both dry and oily in different areas of the face. The most "typical" pattern is the T-pattern, with the oily sections across the forehead and down the nose and chin. Your oily areas might be in different places, such as along your hairline or across your cheeks. You will recognize the oily parts as being more greasy with larger pores than the other areas of your face and the dry sections as being flaky or redder than the other parts of your face. It is that easy.

Unfortunately, there is not really one soap that is good for both kinds of skin so you'll have a slightly more complicated cleansing ritual. Wash each area of your face according to its need — the dry portions with a cleanser that is water based, but also contains the humectants that were mentioned in the section on dry skin, and the oily parts with a water-based cleanser that is more actively drying.

✪ It's also possible to find a non-soap cleanser, which won't clog your pores. Look for ones that are pH balanced and oil-free. If your skin isn't extremely dry or extremely oily, you might be able to use products for "normal" skin. Read the ingredients and experiment. Again, watch your skin's reaction — it will tell you soon enough if you are treating it well.

✪ You might find that you'll need to use a bit of moisturizer on the dry areas of your face — just be careful not to get it on the oily areas. Use a light moisturizer with noncomedogenic (non-clogging) ingredients.

✪ For the oily parts of your face, use blotting tissues or very light (low- or non-alcohol) astringent or toner.

★★★

DO's for combination skin
1. Use different cleansers for the dry and oily areas of your skin.
2. Wash your face three times a day, using only water for one of the washings.
3. Use a gentle moisturizer for the dry areas of your face.
4. Use a light astringent sparingly, or use blotting papers, for the oily parts of your face.
5. Pay attention to your skin's reaction.

DON'Ts for combination skin
1. Don't moisturize your entire face.
2. If you use astringent, don't use it on the dry areas of your face.
3. Don't touch your face unnecessarily during the day.

OILY SKIN

Wash 3 times a day with a gentle, drying soap.

Blot the excess oil off during the day or use a low- or non-alcohol toner.

Don't touch your face unnecessarily.

Pay attention to your skin and how it reacts to different products.

DRY SKIN

Wash 2 times a day with a gentle, moisturizing soap.

Use a light moisturizer if necessary.

Don't touch your face unnecessarily.

Pay attention to your skin and how it reacts to different products.

COMBINATION SKIN

Wash 2-3 times a day with one soap for the dry areas and one for the oily areas.

Blot the oily areas during the day or use a low- or non-alcohol toner; use a light moisturizer on the dry sections only if necessary.

Don't touch your face unnecessarily.

Pay attention to your skin and how it reacts to different products.

OUT, OUT, DARN SPOT!

Melanie knows that Steve and Josh are whispering about her, and the only thing that will save her from their staring will be the homeroom bell. Melanie woke up this morning with two new pimples that are bigger than any she's ever seen. She should have stayed home sick — at least until she grew out of this stage. Can you still go to junior high when you're thirty-five?

Sara hates gym class. It's not that she's not athletic — she loves sports. But undressing in front of everyone is horrible, especially because of the pimples on her back. She's sure no one else ever gets them. "Maybe I can break my arm," she thinks hopefully to herself.

Although Julie can hear her younger brother screaming because she's taking too long in the bathroom, she doesn't care. Every night, she locks herself in and examines her face, squeezing any pimples that might have erupted. She knows she shouldn't, but she couldn't possibly go to school the next day with pimples on her face.

According to television, teen magazines, and the radio, breaking out is one of life's worst disasters.

But don't you believe it. Breaking out is a minor inconvenience for most pre-teens and teenagers–that's all. Don't believe those advertisements that perpetuate the myth that you and only you break out.

It isn't true.

But saying it isn't true doesn't change how you might feel about yourself when your skin breaks out. It's helpful to keep it in perspective and know that most kids your age are going through the same thing. We bet that teen actresses and models and even the cutest boy in your math class all get pimples at some time or another. And they probably feel as self-conscious as you do. You are not alone.

You might have heard this before, that breaking out is only a phase. It's true! And it comes to an end at different times for different people. You won't spend the rest of your life wishing you had a paper bag over your head or hearing your brother call you pizza-face.

Whether you have one pimple, five pimples, or ten pimples, that's not all there is to you. People will still like you and be attracted to you whether your skin is broken-out or not. Most people won't even notice.

Everyone's skin breaks out. It's just a matter of degrees. Some girls have skin that is fairly smooth and have an occasional pimple or blackhead. Others have pimples, blackheads or whiteheads that occur more frequently. Some pre-teens and teens have serious breakouts that won't let up, and for those cases it's best to see a dermatologist for medication and treatment.

As with your type of skin, acne is also hereditary. Although different factors — such as your menstrual cycle, your emotions, allergies, and food — may play a role in the degree and frequency of your breakouts, they are not the main cause of acne.

What are pimples, blackheads, and whiteheads? They are blemishes that erupt due to an overproduction of oil which closes off the pores. This is why people with oily skin tend to have pimples more often than those with dry skin. A blackhead is created when oil in a clogged pore meets the air and the oxygen turns the oil black. A whitehead is oil trapped under the skin where the oxygen cannot get to it, so it doesn't turn black.

Although the whitehead is covered by skin, oil and skin cells are still being produced. Eventually, because other substances are being produced, the whitehead can explode into a pimple.

So, what should you do?

First, ask yourself a few questions. Are you having your period? Are you about to get it? Did you just have it? It's the hormonal changes which occur with the onset of puberty that cause the general increase of oil production. Each time you get your period, hormones are active again and may be causing your skin to break out.

Have you made any other changes in your life? Are you eating different foods, sleeping less, under more stress? You might be allergic to new foods, to a new soap, to a new shampoo. If you are undergoing emotional stress, this too can affect your skin and cause you to break out.

Please, don't feel hopeless — don't feel that your skin is a mess now and nothing can help you. First, see if you can figure out what caused the breakout. If it is an allergic reaction, then you'll know not to use that product anymore or eat that kind of food.

If you get an occasional pimple, let it be. Remember, the best thing is not to touch your skin because if you do, it might cause other pimples to develop. If you leave it alone, it will go away.

If you pick or squeeze your blemish, you will make it worse. You'll only get a small amount of the solidified oil out and the rest will be pushed deeper into your skin, possibly creating a bigger pimple that will last longer. You might even cause a scar. It is best not to touch or fool around with the pimple.

HELP!

There are a zillion different products you can buy to help quicken the disappearing process or help unblock your pores. Look for *salicylic acid* listed in the ingredients because it helps unclog pores. Use these products sparingly because most will have alcohol as another ingredient, and alcohol can really overdry your skin.

✪ There are also creams and gels with *benzoyl peroxide* that dry out the actual blemish. They come mostly in three strengths — two-and-a-half, five, and ten percent. Start with the lowest percentage of benzoyl peroxide, for it might be very irritating to your skin. Watch how your skin reacts; you might want to increase the amount of benzoyl peroxide if it is necessary. Gently place the gel or cream on the pimple and on the surrounding area. Be careful not to dry out your skin. If it turns red, flakes, or burns, stop using the product. As always, listen to what your skin is telling you.

✪ It is hard to say how to prevent pimples. Washing your face properly and gently with the correct soap that doesn't clog your pores or dry out your skin helps. Not touching your face unnecessarily goes a long way in stopping the increase of pimples. Avoiding foods that you are allergic to will help. Even making sure your shampoo is non-irritating to your skin can reduce breakouts.

It is not fun having acne. It can cause embarrassment and misery. Yes, it is right there on your face and if people look for it, they can see it. But it's not all there is to *you*.

If you are truly miserable and if you feel your condition is serious — serious because you're breaking out a lot and it is beyond your control, or serious because you feel awful about yourself — talk to your parents. Ask them if you can go to a dermatologist for professional care.

ASK THE DOCTOR

A dermatologist can determine whether or not your skin condition is serious. The doctor can recommend skin treatment and, if necessary, medication. Don't be afraid to ask the doctor any questions you have about acne, treatment, and about medicine and its side effects. The doctor's there to answer your questions and to help you.

TALK TO YOUR FRIENDS

Breaking out is a very sensitive issue. You might want to pretend it's not happening to you and so not talk about it.

But you'll find that if you talk about your skin and how you feel about it with friends you trust, you'll feel better. You'll probably find that they feel the same way you do—self-conscious and uncomfortable. You might even find out that they think your skin is great and wished theirs looked as good as yours.

Together, you can find ways to cope with pimples and how to take care of them, and then forget about them. Knowing you're not alone can go a long way in making you feel better about yourself.

Life is more than the pimple on your chin and you are more than your skin. Let the beautiful you shine through!

BODY TALK

Your body deserves as much attention as your face. So, whether you take refreshing showers or soothing bubble baths — it's always a good time to baby your skin.

Be gentle with the skin on your body. Wash your body with lukewarm water as much as possible. Yes, it's hard on those really cold days when a hot shower feels great or those broiling summer nights when a cold shower is the only thing that can save you from melting. Instead, take cool baths or showers during the summer and, in the winter, don't let the shower or bath water get so hot that your skin turns red.

While washing, use a soapy washcloth to gently remove dead skin cells. Definitely make sure you rinse off completely.

If you break out on your shoulders, neck, chest, and back, treat that skin as you would your face. Don't use the washcloth there — gently use the same soap you use for your face. If you use any product to dry out the pimples on your face, use it wherever else they appear.

You don't have many oil glands on the soles of your feet or hands, on your knees or elbows, so you might tend to have dry skin there. After your bath or shower, use a light moisturizer. If there are bumps on the backs of your arms and they are not pimples, they are usually due to dryness. After washing, gently massage in a bit of moisturizer. It is best to moisturize when your skin is slightly damp.

TIPS FOR BATHING

If a bath is your best place for thinking, relaxing, or dreaming, make sure the water is between 95 and 105 degrees and that you're in it for only twenty minutes. Baths can dehydrate your skin.

If you take bubble baths or use bath oils, rinse your skin thoroughly after the bath, for the ingredients can irritate your skin, especially your delicate vaginal skin. Bath time is a great time to work on specific spots — like the calluses on your feet or the rough areas of your heels, elbows, and knees— with a pumice stone. Make sure you have been soaking for a while so your skin is soft, making it easier to get your skin into shape.

★★★

DO's for bathing and showering

1. The water temperature should be lukewarm.
2. Gently use a wet, soapy washcloth, removing the dead skin.
3. If your skin is oily, treat your back, shoulders, and chest as you would your face.
4. Remove calluses from your feet after they've been softened by water.
5. After bathing, moisturize the dry areas of your body while your skin is still damp.

DON'Ts for bathing and showering

1. Don't stay in the bath longer than twenty minutes.
2. Don't let the water for your shower or bath be extremely hot or cold.
3. Don't forget to rinse or even wash off any bubble-bath or bath oils after your soak.
4. Don't forget to use the right kind of soap for your skin.

★★★

Giving Yourself the Treatment

*I*magine this.

You walk into a drug store just to buy some soap. As you walk down an aisle, you hear a murmur. You turn down the aisle for skin care products, and the sound gets louder. You hear your name being called.

It's the astringents, demanding that you buy them; the facial scrubs are promising totally clean skin. The moisturizers are jumping down from the shelves, dancing around your feet, offering smooth, soft skin. The boxes of facial masks are pushing the astringents out of the way to get closer to you. Suddenly the whole aisle is alive, each product demanding that you pick it.

You try to back away, but you're surrounded on all sides.

"Help," you scream. "What should I buy?"

Whoa! Stop this nightmare! Wake up!

Does this sound familiar? Do you feel this way when you go into a drug store and try to decide which product would actually be good for your skin? Do you wonder if the products can actually do what they claim?

☆☆ QUIZ ☆☆

Before you even read this chapter, take the following true/false quiz.

1. *Astringents and masks decrease the size of your pores.*
   True or False
2. *Steaming your face gets the oil out of your pores.*
   True or False
3. *Moisturizing prevents wrinkling.*
   True or False
4. *The more grainy the facial scrub, the cleaner your face will be.*
   True or False
5. *Products that claim they get "down deep" into your pores are good for your skin.*
   True or False
6. *In order to have really smooth, clean skin, open the pores to clean them and then close them to make sure nothing harmful gets in.*
   True or False

7. *Masks are a necessary part of your cleaning ritual.*
   True or False
8. *Moisturizers feed your skin from the outside, adding the necessary oils your skin needs.*
   True or False
9. *The healthiest and cleanest feeling is that tingly sensation you get from washing or using astringents, masks and facial scrubs.*
   True or False
10. *The more alcohol in a product, the better it is for you.*
    True or False

☆☆☆

As you might have guessed, none of these statements are true. It would be super if some of them were true, such as the ability to shrink one's pores, but unfortunately it isn't. On the other hand, knowing the truth will save you money, time, and your skin.

This chapter is about all the skin care products and treatments on the market. You'll learn what each product does or doesn't do, the different kinds available, and who should use them.

One note before you start. As a general rule, never buy perfumed or scented skin care products. It's an added ingredient that may be irritating to your skin.

ASTRINGENTS

Manufacturers make a lot of claims about what astringents, toners, or tonics can do. The cold truth is that they remove the oil and dead skin cells that sit on top of your skin. Washing your face does the same job without any of the bad side effects such as stinging, drying and redness.

Most astringents are made up of alcohol, water, and fragrance. Fragrance and alcohol can be irritating to your skin so avoid using them. Using too much or too harsh an astringent can cause the oil glands to over-produce oil to make up for the effect of the astringent — and this is the opposite of what you're trying to accomplish! Astringents can also dry out your top layer of skin to the point of flakiness and redness.

Contrary to popular belief, astringents don't shrink pores; your pores may look smaller after you use an astringent, but that is only temporary. It also doesn't go deep within your pores and clean them out — it only cleans the surface of your skin.

One of the reported jobs of an astringent is to remove the excess soap or cleanser film you have on your face after you wash it. If you use the correct facial soap and rinse properly, you won't need an astringent to remove anything — your face will be totally clean already.

It's hard to believe that astringents are a necessary part of facial care. If you use them, use unscented astringents with no or very little alcohol content—and use them sparingly!

We don't recommend using astringents on dry skin but you can try a gentle one when you are unable to wash your face during the day and need to remove some of the excess oil, or in the hot, humid months of summer when your skin produces even more oil.

As always, pay attention to how your skin reacts to the product. If it starts getting red, flaky, or dry, you'll know you have overused your astringent. The tingly feeling that you sometimes experience with astringent might be the very hint that tells you that your skin is reacting badly to it. If your skin is sensitive stay away from astringents because sensitive skin might break out in a rash or overreact to the ingredients.

MOISTURIZERS

Along with astringents, moisturizers are some of the most used and most misunderstood products.

Basically, moisturizers help bind water to the skin and cut down the dryness on the surface. They smooth and soften your outer skin — at least temporarily. You aren't adding oil to your skin.

Moisturizers come in cream or lotion form. Lotions have a higher percentage of water and are called lighter moisturizers. Creams have less water and are considered to be heavier moisturizers.

You might not need to use a moisturizer. Only use one if your skin is dry, red, or flaky.

━━━━━━━━━━ **POP QUIZ** ━━━━━━━━━━

Before you run out and buy a moisturizer, check and see what else you are presently doing to your skin. Is your soap too drying? If you use astringent, is it too harsh? Do you need an astringent?

If you answered no, no, and no, then moisturizers may be for you.

Choose an oil-free or water-based moisturizer, for the heavier the moisturizer, the more it clogs pores. Look for a noncomedogenic (non-clogging) moisturizer. The ingredients in this type of moisturizer would most likely be glycerin, lactic acid, propylene glycol. Cottonseed oil, sodium lauryl sulfate, and isotearyl neopentate are also good ingredients.

Avoid moisturizers that list heavy mineral oil, lanolin, or petrolatum (petroleum jelly). You don't want to clog your pores and cause breakouts. As always, avoid products with fragrance.

Some moisturizers have many other ingredients, which do nothing useful for your skin and just cost more. It hasn't been proven that eggs, milk, honey, proteins, elastin, or amino acids do anything for your skin.

Use moisturizer on the drier parts of your body such as your heels, elbows, and knees. For those areas, you can use a heavier moisturizer, since you don't have to worry about clogging up those pores.

HOW TO APPLY MOISTURIZER

1. Wash your face.
2. Spray your face with a light mist of water and gently spread the moisturizer on your face.
3. Gently dab off the excess lotion with a tissue.

Some people believe you should only use it at night. Try that and if your skin is still dry, you might want to use it after you wash your face in the morning.

FACIAL SCRUBS AND ABRASIVES

Some people believe that facial scrubs are good for the skin because they slough off dead skin, giving the living skin a chance to breathe. They also say that facial scrubs clean out your pores which can help keep them from clogging.

The problem is — how does the facial scrub know which skin cells are dead and which are alive? And if the facial scrub is deep-cleaning your pores, what else is it doing?

If facial scrubs and abrasives deep-clean your skin, going way into your pores, won't your face bleed? Gross! Not quite the look you want.

Also, you know you're supposed to treat your skin gently and lovingly and using something called an abrasive doesn't sound very gentle, does it?

So... what does it all mean?

You do have dead skin cells that need to come off but you don't want to be abusive to your skin. And your entire face isn't covered with clogged pores. The best bet is to use something gentle and even-grained every once in a while— certainly not every day, and not everywhere.

The best facial scrub is baking soda. It is gentle and fine-grained and inexpensive. And your mom is sure to have some right in the kitchen!

The baking soda gently sloughs off the dead skin cells, unblocking pores without irritating your skin.

A BAKING SODA SCRUB

1. After you wash your face, take one tablespoon of baking soda in your palm, and one tablespoon of water, and apply the mixture to wherever there are blackheads or whiteheads. Gently rub! Rinse off with lukewarm water.
2. If you have oily skin, you might use the baking soda over your whole face, gently massaging it on your skin, avoiding the area around your eyes, which is very delicate and sensitive.
3. Use the baking soda once and see how your skin reacts to it. If it turns too red or dries out, perhaps you've rubbed too harshly or your skin might be too sensitive.*

FACIAL MASKS

Another tricky area. Manufacturers claim that masks can soften your skin, tighten skin, stimulate skin, exfoliate skin, absorb oils, close up pores, and smooth out skin all while you're doing your homework, your laundry and practicing the flute. Sounds too good to be true!

Here are the facts: Masks can clean skin and can remove excess oil and perhaps moisturize and smooth skin—temporarily. It is not clear that masks do anything that a basic, good cleaning ritual can't do.

And, if you use a mask too often, it may cause broken blood vessels or if it is the wrong type, it may cause more damage than good.

Before getting involved with facial masks, remember that these skin treatments are primarily for older women and aren't necessary for your skin right now.

* *Seventeen*, October 1987, p. 56

How to Apply a Facial Mask

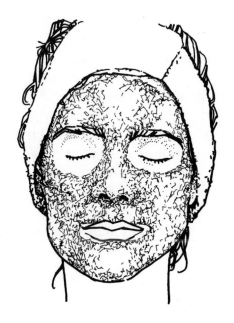

There are basically two types of masks — paste masks for oily skin and cream masks for dry skin.

The cream masks have oil, wax and water and, in effect, moisturize the skin. They may also feel refreshing.

The paste masks have a more powdery base and some contain ingredients such as apricot pits, almond meal, oats, bran, and clay. These also refresh the skin and perhaps aid circulation, and they absorb oil. They also might abrade the skin a bit (apricot pits sound somewhat harsh). Clay masks are smoother and less abrasive and, at the same time, absorb oil.

If you have dry skin, look for a mask containing

creams (and some of the same ingredients you find when you would look for a moisturizer). If you have oily skin, stick to a clay mask. Everyone should avoid masks with fragrances in them.

Before you use a mask, wash your face thoroughly. Make sure you do not put the mask on your lips, nostrils, or the delicate skin around your eyes. The mask should only come down to right above your eyebrows and start where your cheekbones are, leaving a big clear circle around your eyes.

Again, it is not proven that masks do anything useful and in some cases (if your skin is sensitive or if you're using the wrong kind), it may cause you to break out more, dry your skin, or cause a rash. Check with your mom or your doctor before using a mask.

STEAMING

Steaming is another area of conflicting information. According to some, steaming opens your pores and cleanses them, allowing oils to pour out. Others believe that steaming is only good for your sweat glands, opening up those pores, while closing the oil pores. And other experts have said that pores don't open and close — or else each would have a muscle attached to it, enabling it to move.

Steaming does soften the outer layer of skin. Dermatologists and cosmetologists use steaming to soften the skin in order to help them remove blackheads, whiteheads, and pimples. But these are professionals who know how to properly remove these blemishes from the face and that's something that you should not do. Trying to squeeze or pop pimples and blackheads is asking for trouble. You could make the condition much worse.

Steaming is really not necessary. Before you consider it, talk to your mom or your doctor. Never attempt steaming on your own.

ADVERTISING

Some products claim that they have "natural" ingredients and therefore must be better than any products which don't make this claim. Just because something is natural doesn't mean it's good for you. Also, check out the list of ingredients. Is this natural substance one of the first five ingredients? If not, then there isn't much in the product.

Some products claim that they are "hypoallergenic," which means they probably don't contain fragrances or perfumes. Otherwise, they are fairly similar to the other products on the market.

Do check the ingredients. Stay away from products with perfumes. See if you are paying extra for "natural" ingredients when the amount is so small it probably doesn't have any effect.

FACTS, ONLY THE FACTS

- Steaming, astringents, and facial masks cannot alter the size of your pores.
- Moisturizers help retain your skin's moisture.
- Dry skin doesn't mean early wrinkles, and moisturizers will not stop nature's path.
- "New improved," "natural," and "organic" don't necessarily mean that the product is special or better than other products on the shelves.
- Astringents remove only excess, surface oil.
- Tingly skin can mean irritated skin.

Living In
Your Skin

E mma is a sports nut. Whatever the season, she's
out there biking, swimming, skiing, skating. While
this is great for her body, she's noticing that her skin
isn't reacting as well.

She has dry skin and all the chlorine, cold, and sun
are drying out her skin even more. So Emma started
using moisturizer to counteract the dryness.

To her horror, she started breaking out, getting
whiteheads. She'd never had this problem before so
she started using astringents and harsh soaps, which

dried out her skin even more. She doesn't want to give up her sports, but she is also very self-conscious about her skin.

Tara has a different problem. She has oily skin and during the summers she's a mother's helper at a swim club, which means she's always outside. She knows the sun isn't good for her so she wears sunscreen. But the sunscreen is making her skin more oily, and she's getting more pimples. She's tempted to forgo the sunscreen since she's heard the sun dries out pimples, but what about the harmful effects of the rays?

Ellen knows she has the biggest problem of all. Finally, she's going out with Bob, the boy from orchestra whom she's been chasing all year. And from out of the blue, she has pimples — very obvious ones — on her chin. How could this happen now, right before the date of her life!

Emma, Tara, and Ellen want to know what's going on. They thought skin quality was hereditary and that nothing would affect it. But that's not true. The outside environment and your emotions both affect your skin.

It's true that your *basic* skin quality is hereditary, but skin reacts to what's going on outside and inside. To keep your skin healthy and clear, you have to stand up to your skin and let it know who's the boss.

In this chapter we'll show you how to do just that.

YOUR MENSTRUAL CYCLE

Your body is an interconnected system. If there is a change in one area, the rest of your body will mirror it.

Because of the change in your hormonal balance which activates your menstrual cycle, you might tend to break out more before, during, or after your period.

Use topical medications on the pimples that erupt and decrease the amount of salty, spicy, and fatty foods you eat before your period and see if that helps. Remember that although you get your period every month, it doesn't necessarily mean that you'll break out every month.

Women are affected by their periods in different ways. As you grow up, you'll notice that the cramps, breakouts, or backaches change. It's also very possible that you won't suffer from these symptoms at all.

Getting your period is one of the most obvious signs that you are growing up and becoming a young woman; as you get older, you'll learn how your body changes and what it needs during this cycle.

BE HAPPY, LOOK GREAT

People in love glow. They are happy and that inner joy is radiated out, lighting up their eyes, smile, and skin.

Think about yourself for a moment. Think of specific days recently when you've been really happy and pleased with yourself: maybe you just won a prize, starred in a school play, had a terrific birthday party, or just a great day hanging out with your friends. Your skin probably reflected your inner feelings and shone with health. It's definitely true that if you feel good, you look good. And as the song says, "You're as beautiful as you feel!"

The opposite is also true. If you're feeling sick, you'll look pale, perhaps even gray. Or if you're upset, sad, or angry, your skin will reflect that.

You can easily deal with the specific skin problem that develops—drying out your pimples, moisturizing, exercising, eating healthily.

But most important, you need to take care of what is upsetting you. When you're feeling sad, angry, or upset, talk to people — friends, parents, sisters, teachers, whomever you feel most comfortable with. It's not the time to retreat into yourself. Share your feelings and you will begin to feel better.

The faster you take care of yourself emotionally, the faster your skin will regain its healthy, clear glow.

CLIMATE CONTROL

The weather can affect your skin. So it's best to prepare your skin to thrive in all seasons.

A WINTER WONDERLAND

Winter is the season for sledding and for curling up by a fire. Winter is also a season of extremes. It can be both very dry and very cold. Inside your home or school you might be very warm, but step outside and you are suddenly faced with freezing cold weather. All these extremes and changes can be tricky for your skin.

People with dry and sensitive skin must be especially careful during the winter months. The low humidity and cold are excessively drying to your skin, sucking the moisture out of it, causing blotchy, red, flaky skin and chapped lips.

When you're outdoors skiing, skating, or just walking, there are several things you can do to protect yourself:

✪ Wear a scarf around your face to protect your skin from the wind and cold.

✪ Moisturize your skin with a light moisturizer whenever it feels dry. Be careful not to add clogged pores to your overly dry skin by using too heavy (oily) or too much moisturizer. Use moisturizers with humectants listed in the ingredients (propylene glycol and glycerin) for they draw moisture to the skin.

The capillaries (tiny veins) in your face contract from the cold outside and expand from the indoor heat. Sometimes, the veins can't handle the constant expansion and contraction, and they break, forming lasting red splotches or just redness on your skin. Using a scarf or moisturizer can help protect you.

✪ Hot baths feel wonderful in the winter, but they dehydrate your skin so space them out and make sure you use moisturizer.

✪ Use a humidifier to combat the drying effects of indoor heating. Talk to your parents about the advantages of a humidifier. It's good for your skin and for helping you breathe more comfortably.

If you have oily skin, it's equally important for you to protect your skin, because cold, lack of humidity, and heat will affect you also:

✪ Be careful not to block your pores if you use a

moisturizer. Choose one that is water-based and that has humectants as its main ingredients. Don't use moisturizers on your face that have lanolin, mineral oil, wax, or other heavy oils.

✪ Lightly spray mineral water on your face, then use a light moisturizer, and gently blot off the excess lotion and water.

✪ Winter is the time when you wear your beautiful wool sweaters, and the layered look is warm as well as fashionable. Wear cotton close to your skin to absorb perspiration— otherwise the sweat can irritate your skin, causing breakouts, especially on your chest, shoulders, and back. Hats and scarves can rub against your face, causing irritation. Once you're indoors, blot your skin to remove the excess oil. Make sure you wash your back, shoulders, and chest and treat them as carefully and gently as you would your face.

LIPS

Chapped lips are the curse of the winter months so use a lip ointment or lip gloss, making sure it contains sunscreen to keep your lips soft and moist. If you wear lipstick, apply lip ointment first and then put on your lipstick. Licking your lips does not keep your lips smooth and soft; it dries them even more.

HOT TIMES

Glorious summer, with its long, slow days, beach parties, barbecues, and picnics, is a time of fun and freedom!

It's also when you need to protect your skin from the hot, humid, sunny weather so you can enjoy the summer fully. The humidity and heat cause sweat and oil glands to work overtime, resulting in excess clogging of the pores, especially for people with oily or combination skin. The best thing to do is to blot your skin gently with blotting paper tissues and make sure you wash your face two to three times a day. If you use an astringent, make sure it is a low- or non-alcohol-based astringent for alcohol is too harsh and too drying for your skin, especially during the summer months.

Dry skin reacts much better to summer heat and moisture, for the weather is less drying, but your skin might be more sensitive to the sun. Be doubly sure that your moisturizer is water based; don't clog your pores with heavy oils.

HERE COMES THE SUN

Everybody loves the sun, and when summer comes outdoors is the only place to be. You can have lots of fun in the sun if you take the right precautions.

As everyone knows by now, the sun can be extremely harmful to your skin. Besides the pain of sunburn, overexposure to the sun can cause early aging and wrinkling of the skin, leathery skin texture, discolorations, and broken blood vessels as well as cancer. Whether it's winter or summer, you have to be careful of the dangerous effects of the sun's rays. Although your sunburn might go away and your suntan fades, the damage caused by the sun does not.

A golden tan does not mean health. And what happens to you when you're young will affect your skin later on.

The winter sun is less strong, but you can still get burned. Whether you're skiing down a mountain, skating on a pond, or even shoveling the driveway, use a sunscreen, for the sun reflects off of the snow.

When you buy a sunblock, pay attention to the sun protection factor (SPF) and buy one that is strong enough to protect your skin, depending on how sensitive your skin is and how fair you are. It is better to be overprotected than to burn. Buy a sunscreen that blocks out both UVB rays (which cause sunburn on the upper skin layers) and UVA rays (which damage the deeper layers of skin).

SPF refers to the amount of time you can spend in the sun without getting burned. Using a lotion labeled SPF 15 enables you to stay in the sun fifteen times as long as you normally can without a sunscreen.

If you have oily skin, use an oil-free sunblock. With dry skin, you might want to try a sunblock with moisturizer. If you notice blackheads or whiteheads, switch to an oil-free sunblock.

Always use a sunscreen. Don't think you can go outside and, an hour later, apply the first coat of sunscreen. The sun isn't waiting and neither should you. Put the sunscreen on half an hour before you go outside and reapply the lotion every two to three hours, especially if you are sweating heavily or playing sports. If you are swimming, put some on before you go in and after you get out of the water.

The sun is the strongest between 10 A. M. and 3 P. M. You don't have to hide in the basement with your brother's spider collection during these hours, just make sure you are wearing a strong enough sunblock.

Wearing protective clothing is great, but the lighter the fabric or the more you can see through it, the easier it is for the sun's harmful rays to get through it, too. So, although it would be lovely to think you are protecting yourself wearing pretty, gauzy clothes and sheer bathing suit coverups, you really aren't.

The water and sand reflect the sun's rays. Sitting under a beach umbrella doesn't shield you from the sun.

A cloudy day is just as dangerous as a clear day, for the sun's ultraviolet rays easily reach you through the clouds.

Buy lip ointment that contains sunscreen with a high SPF number. Licking your lips increases the effect of the sun's ultraviolet rays and increases chapping, burning, and cracking.

MYTH

The sun will not clear up your pimples. Under the heat of the sun, your skin will start producing more oil in reaction to the drying powers of the sun. But once you are out of the sun, it takes a while for your skin to slow down the procedure. With the increase of oil, sweat, and suntan lotion, your pores will begin to clog and create pimples.

You will also develop more whiteheads, which will appear four to six weeks after your exposure to the sun. The ultraviolet radiation from the sun causes the pores to clog under the skin's surface.

The sun is not a friend to skin. Golden tans are lovely to look at, but the damage that the sun causes is too high a cost to pay. Respect yourself and take care of your skin now.

Be a smart alabaster beauty instead of a dumb, bronzed one!

SUNGLASSES

Your eyes and the skin around your eyes need special attention. The best kind of glasses should protect your eyes from UVA and UVB rays. The best colors for your lenses are gray, green, brown, and amber. Blue, black, and pink — although they may look good — don't do anything to filter out the sun's harmful rays.

FOOD, GLORIOUS FOOD

The question you've been waiting for: Do chocolate, soda, hamburgers, french fries, and potato chips cause pimples and greasy skin?

The answer is — *TA –DA* — maybe not. There is no proven correlation between the foods a person eats and the condition of her skin.

STOP! Don't run out and eat everything in sight! Becoming a junk-food blimp is not the answer or the way to get the boy of your dreams!

If you eat unhealthy foods, it will show up in the quality and look of your skin. You cannot fuel yourself with low quality and non-nutritious foods and expect your body to run and look as if you are taking good care of it. Your skin will reflect what you eat, but the foods themselves don't necessarily give you pimples or oily skin.

FOOD GROUPS

There are four basic food groups — vegetables/fruit, bread and cereal, dairy, and meat — and to eat healthily, you need to eat a certain amount each day from each group.

Two servings a day should come from the meat group. Meat includes beef, poultry, fish, beans (soybeans, tofu), and nuts.

Four servings should come from the dairy group (milk, cheese).

One thing to remember about the two groups above is that these foods contain a lot of fat. No matter what your skin type, fat is not healthy for you. Although there is no proof, it is believed that if you have less fat in your diet, your skin might look healthier.

There are different ways to decrease the amount of fat in your diet without giving up the healthy and necessary foods you need.

Peanut butter (part of the meat group because of the nuts) is high in fat. You can buy low-fat or partially defatted peanut butter. You can also "defat" your own by buying natural peanut butter and pouring the excess fat off. Keep the jar in the refrigerator after you use it; it will keep fresh longer.

SEVEN WAYS TO CUT OUT FAT

1. Drink low-fat milk rather than whole milk.
2. Eat nonfat yogurt instead of low-fat yogurt.
3. Use margarine instead of butter.
4. Use mustard instead of mayonnaise.
5. Order mushrooms on your pizza rather than pepperoni or sausage.
6. Use diet dressing (or lemon with pepper or other herbs) instead of regular dressing on salads.
7. Put one slice of cheese in your sandwich rather than more.

FOUR WAYS TO TELL IF YOUR FOOD IS FATTY

1. The softer the cookie, the more fat.
2. The cheaper the food, the more fat.
3. The shinier the food, the more fat.
4. The moister the cake, the more fat.

Include in your diet four servings a day from the fruits and vegetables group. The greener the vegetable, the healthier it is. And don't forget to include yellow vegetables in your diet. The fresher the fruit or vegetable, the better (it is better to eat fresh rather than canned fruit, and "fresh-frozen" rather than frozen vegetables). Steam your vegetables with the lid on the pot, which will keep the nutrients in.

Lastly, you need four servings a day from the breads and cereal group (pasta, rice, grains). To do the most good, these foods should be whole-grained foods, not refined or processed. For example, whole wheat bread is more healthful than white bread.

Spicy foods and shellfish may also be foods that promote breakouts, but it is not proven. You might want to try cutting those kinds of foods out of your diet for a while and see what happens.

Salt and sugar — although they taste wonderful — are not healthy for you in excess. Salt retains water, and you will get enough sugar and salt naturally from the healthy foods you are eating without adding them at the table.

There might be foods in your diet that you are allergic to. One way to figure this out is to cut out the food that you believe is causing the problem — rash, hives, or breakouts — and see how your skin reacts. Also, talk with your parents and see if you need to check this out with a doctor.

"BUT I LOVE JUNK FOOD!"

It might be hard to change the way you eat for a number of reasons. First, you are not the only one in your home. You can't stop cookies, canned foods, and whole milk from coming into your house and tempting you. It is also difficult to protest and refuse to eat what you're being served. Boycotting in your own home is not always a good policy.

Talk with your parents if you decide that the food served is not always the food you want to eat. You can explain that you are trying to cut down on certain types of foods and to add other kinds (like fresh vegetables or low-fat milk) to your diet. Perhaps your changing the way you eat will be helpful to the rest of the family.

Second, it sometimes seems that the best tasting foods are the ones that are the least good for you. Pizzas with everything on them and soft cookies are delicious and potato chips are addicting no matter what anyone says. It's also especially difficult to avoid these treats if everyone around you is eating the very food that you would sell your younger brother for.

Don't be fanatical about this. Be easy on yourself. If you end up eating sweets or too many french fries, don't be angry with yourself. You did it. It's not the end of the world and it doesn't mean you have to eat that way the next day.

You want to eat healthily, not starve or punish yourself. There is a difference. If you are unsure about what foods do what, ask your parents, a teacher, or a doctor, or go to the library. Be good to yourself — eat good food to feel good and look good. If you don't know what's the best food program for you, ask your mom for advice or ask your doctor.

Before you faint from all this info, remember, you don't have to change your life and all your eating habits in one day; it's okay to treat yourself to your favorite foods once in a while.

WATER, WATER EVERYWHERE

Water! Remember how important it is for you to find a soap or cleansing lotion with water as a main in-gredient. It is equally important that you drink six to eight glasses of water a day. Pure, clean water is a must for a healthy body and skin. Water cleans you both inside and out. You are made up mostly of water and need to replenish yourself. Soda and fruit juices are not the same and can't replace water. Space out your water intake through the day so you don't feel bloated.

THE SPORTING SCENE

You've all seen those science fiction movies where the alien creatures are only heads or brains — pure intellect — and they want our human bodies.

They're after us because they know the importance and joy of being physical, moving around, having fun. Without bodies, they can't know the thrill of skiing, the joy of dancing, the fun of tennis, the pleasure of swimming. They know their race made a major mistake when they decided to get rid of their bodies.

These aliens are not stupid!

Luckily, we still have our bodies — and they crave exercise and movement.

Our bodies know what's good for them.

Exercise does so much for you. It reduces stress and gets your heart and lungs working, giving oxygen to your whole body, making your skin glow with health. Good muscle tone, which comes with regular exercise, also enriches your skin's appearance.

Caring for your skin before and after you exercise reduces the risk of skin problems. Always exercise with a clean face, no makeup, and with your hair pulled back. Because you sweat as you exercise, you want to perspire as easily as possible without anything blocking the pores. Also, if you are sweating a lot, your makeup will run. Really gross! You will look better with a freshly washed, clean face.

RUNNING, TENNIS, BIKING, DANCING, AEROBICS

All these activities have sweating in common — great!

● If you use a sweatband, make sure it is always clean before you start your exercise.

● If you have oily skin, bring along blotting tissues or non-alcohol astringent pads to wipe the excess sweat and oil away when you finish.

● If you are doing these activities outside, you'll need a sunscreen. Use one that is oil-free, especially if you have oily skin.

● You might want to use a special eye stick with sunscreen in it for the area around your eyes — it's painful when sunscreen lotion drips into your eyes. Wear a visor so you won't squint the entire time.

SKIING, SKATING, SLEDDING

Winter outdoor activities pose their own problems.

✪ If you have dry skin, use a sunscreen with a moisturizer.

✪ If you have oily skin, you probably will do best with a non-oil or water-based sunscreen.

✪ Protect the skin around your eyes with a light moisturizer under your eye stick sunscreen — especially if you have dry skin.

✪ Remember that baths are dehydrating and your skin will be dehydrated from being in the sun, cold, and wind. You do want to clean your skin from the sunscreen and sweat so it's better to shower and moisturize afterwards.

SWIMMING

Swimming is another sport that can dry out your skin.

✪ As with the other sports, make sure you are clean before you swim. If you have fresh water on your skin, the chlorine or salt won't dry it out as much.

✪ If you are outside, wear a sunscreen, putting it on before and after you swim.

✪ After you shower, moisturize your whole body as well as your face if you have dry skin. If you have oily skin or combination skin, see how your body and face feel. Be aware that your back, shoulders and chest might react as your face does and might not need as much of the light moisturizer as the rest of your body does.

SWEET DREAMS

Sleep is vital for clear, healthy-looking skin. If your body is exhausted, your skin will look exhausted too —pale, sallow, or just drawn-looking. Everyone needs a different amount of sleep; just make sure you get what you need.

SMOKED OUT

As everyone knows, smoking is very bad for you. It is also very bad for your skin. It discolors your skin and ages it, causing more wrinkles and sagging earlier in life.

SMOKING KILLS and it can also make you ugly! So, to look good and live longer, *DON'T SMOKE!*

☆☆ THE ULTIMATE QUIZ ☆☆

So now you know everything you need to know. If you were suddenly whisked off to Iceland or Tahiti, would you know how to care for your skin? Of course you would.

In case you're unsure, take the following test. If you get a high score, you know you'll look great wherever you are.

1. *You're offered your choice of french fries, soaked in catsup and salt, or a bag of organic carrot sticks, washed, but not scraped. You:*

    a. Lunge for the french fries, knowing that tomorrow's another day.

b. Eat the boring carrots, knowing your eyes and skin will be eternally grateful to you.

c. Say no to both, and offer the new cute guy in your English class some of your homemade, healthy muffins and jam.

2. *You're finally at the beach with the coolest group from school, but no one — absolutely no one — is putting on any sunscreen. You:*

   a. Calmly take yours out and put it on whenever you need to, and ask if anyone wants to borrow some.

   b. Finally sneak into the girls' changing room and spread some on.

   c. Push yours to the bottom of your bag and talk yourself into believing that one day of burn can't hurt — too much.

3. *Your current crush has invited you to do some serious biking with him as part of an early-morning exercise routine. Do you:*

   a. Say no — there's no way you would let anyone see you at that time, especially without makeup?

   b. Skip breakfast and put on your latest outfit, complete with makeup and jewelry?

   c. Meet him wearing no makeup on your freshly-washed face, but looking great in your black leggings and magenta T-shirt?

4. *You're depressed. Everyone but you is at the hottest concert in town. You:*

   a. Eat everything in the house, edible or not.

   b. Put on some records, experiment with your makeup and hair and pretend you're a rock star.

c. Make lists of all the injustices in the world, with your not being allowed to go to the concert at the top.

5. *You just got your period and three new pimples. In two days, you are about to have the biggest party of your life at your house. You:*

   a. Change the party to a costume party so you can wear the seven veils of Salome — over your face.

   b. Attack those pimples by squeezing them into submission, knowing you can repeat the process next week when they come back.

   c. Use the topical medications you have now and plan on using special eye makeup that night to focus everyone's attention on your beautiful baby blues.

Add up your score.

1.	a - 1 point	4.	a - 1 point
	b - 2 points		b - 3 points
	c - 3 points		c - 2 points

2.	a - 3 points	5.	a - 2 points
	b - 2 points		b - 1 point
	c - 1 point		c - 3 points

3.	a - 2 points
	b - 1 point
	c - 3 points

If you scored 5-8, it's time to read this book again. Looking good and being cool are important, but even the wildest girl in your school wouldn't go this far.

If you scored 10-12, at least you're not hurting yourself, but you're not being yourself and probably not even having fun.

If you scored 13-15, you get the good skin seal of approval. You know what's good for you.

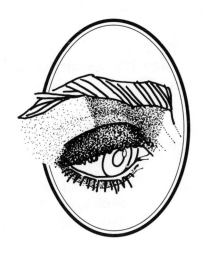

To Make Up or Not to Make Up

You're now a pro at taking care of your skin. You have a simple and complete routine of skin care. Now what?

To make up or not to make up — that is the question. And we're not talking about lovers' quarrels here; we're talking about blush, lip gloss, and eyeshadow!

Do you want to look glamorous, be a natural beauty, or sizzle with a really hot look? Perhaps the no-makeup look is the one for you.

To wear makeup or not is definitely a personal question. It is also an issue that involves your parents and your friends. First decide what *you* want before worrying about what your friends are doing. Then talk to your mom. Then add up the pros and cons.

☆☆ QUIZ ☆☆

The following quiz will help you decide what makeup approach you're most comfortable with. Are you a Makeup Maven, a Fresh-Faced Femme Fatale, or an Artless Angel?

1. *In the mornings:*
    a. I'm barely awake enough to make it to the front door.
    b. I set aside an hour to put on my makeup — all of it.
    c. I go running, shower, dress, and put on lip gloss.
2. *When I go out on a date:*
    a. I put on my new pair of sneakers.
    b. I wear my usual amount of makeup and add my glittery eyeshadow and gold mascara.
    c. I put on my darker lip gloss and a touch of mascara.
3. *Walking down the makeup aisle in a drug store:*
    a. I usually hyperventilate.
    b. I can name every lipstick, eyeshadow, and nail polish just by looking at the color.
    c. I buy my favorite eyeshadow and try a new color.

4. *During lunch at school:*
   a. I'm in the cafeteria eating, where else?
   b. I'm in the girls' room, reapplying my makeup, of course.
   c. I'm hanging out with my friends.
5. *Going out of the house, I feel naked when:*
   a. I'm not wearing my sneakers.
   b. I'm not wearing blush, eyeshadow, mascara, and lip gloss.
   c. I'm not wearing any clothes.
6. *On a camping trip, the most important part of my equipment is:*
   a. Tent, sleeping bag, and my Swiss army knife.
   b. My makeup case and self-lighting mirror.
   c. Food, tent, sunscreen.

Now, to calculate.

✪ If you chose mostly "a," the Artless Angel, then perhaps it's not quite time for you to wear makeup — it doesn't seem to be a priority for you. It also could be that makeup is a little scary. It takes time to learn about makeup and get used to the idea of wearing it. So although you might not want to wear makeup now, that could change. And don't let your fear of the unknown stop you.

✪ A "b" kind of girl — a Makeup Maven — is practically wedded to her makeup. You might not even answer the door without makeup on. You're definitely comfortable wearing makeup, but you might experiment going without makeup some days and letting your natural beauty shine through.

✪ Calling all Fresh-Faced Femme Fatales, if "c" seemed to fit you the most. You like makeup and wear a minimum amount to school and add more when you go out on special dates. You are equally comfortable with or without makeup, depending on how you feel.

☆☆☆

Whichever type fits you, you can always change your mind about makeup. If you decide to wear it some days, it doesn't mean that you are obligated to wear it every day. This is all up to you. If you are most comfortable not wearing makeup, then be a natural beauty!

If most of your friends or girls in your grade are wearing makeup, it might be difficult being one of the few not wearing any. But do what makes you the most comfortable — wearing some so you won't feel different or not wearing any because you don't want to. It is up to you. Makeup is not a life or death issue! If you have a big sister or older cousin, you may want to talk to her about how she felt about makeup when she was your age. And there's always your mom — she's always there to answer questions and give advice — and she'll probably also set some ground rules. That's what moms are for!

What are the makeup rules at your house? Will your parents allow you to wear makeup? What kind? How much? What do you do if your idea of proper makeup is not their idea?

Talk with your parents. Explain to them why you

want to wear makeup and what kind. If you only want to wear makeup when you go out on dates or on special occasions, tell them that. If you want to wear a certain amount each day, explain that to them. What do you want to wear — lip gloss, blush, eyeshadow, mascara?

Listen to what your parents have to say. They may say it's fine. They might want you to wear makeup only at certain times. Be willing to compromise. Offer other suggestions. If they are against your wearing makeup at all, ask them if it is okay to wear it only when you go out on special occasions. If they don't want you wearing lipstick, mascara, and blush, decide which is most important to you and ask if you can wear that only. Or change from lipstick to lip gloss.

If they say no, you'll have to accept that decision. You are still their daughter and under their care. Don't be too upset. Other girls have the same difficulties. There will come a time when you will be able to wear makeup.

MAGAZINE ADS AND HYPE

Before you start learning about makeup and despairing that you will never be as beautiful as the models in the magazines, remember this: These are advertisements — they are not real.

These models' jobs are to look perfect; they have experts styling their hair and putting on their makeup. If that weren't enough, they have professional photographers setting up the lights to make them look their best and then the photographs are retouched so that the girls look perfect with no visible flaws. This is not real!

It also takes hours to set up a professional photo shoot. If you spent that much time on your makeup, you wouldn't have time for hanging out with your friends, teasing your younger sister, doing your homework, or being on the girls' basketball team.

Ads are geared to make you feel that you don't look as wonderful as the model so that you will buy the product. There is no way you can compare yourself to a model in an ad. Look the best you can and feel good about yourself. That's real!

GEARING UP

There are certain items that are good to have when you are putting on makeup. If you don't have them all now, don't worry. As you get older and decide what kind of makeup you want, you'll gather the necessary tools. Right now, start with the basics.

1. You need a mirror, preferably one that stands up on its own so you don't need to hold it. It could be the mirror in your bathroom or bedroom if there is enough light.
2. Cotton balls.
3. Cotton swabs.
4. Don't spend money on extra brushes or applicators. Everything you need is provided with the makeup you buy.
5. A small makeup case is handy to have for home use, or to put in your purse, back pack, or suitcase.

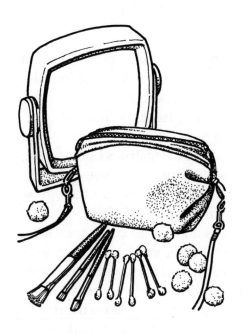

MIRROR, MIRROR ON THE WALL

Now, before you start making up your face, take a look at yourself in the mirror. Write down which feature you like the best.

- ✪ Is it your eyes? Their shape? Color? Your long lashes?
- ✪ Do you like how your brows complement your eyes?
- ✪ Is the shape of your nose interesting, strong, petite?
- ✪ Is your complexion your favorite feature?
- ✪ What about your cheekbones? Are they high and prominent?
- ✪ Do you like the shape of your mouth? The color?
- ✪ Are you pleased with the overall proportion of your face? Do all your features work well with each other?

Focus on what makes you feel good about yourself. These are the features you will highlight.

Then see what parts of your face you are not in love with. Are these features that you can liven up with some color?

If the individual features bother you, try to envision your face without them. You might think that your brows are too bushy, but do they go with your face? Would thin brows look funny? If your nose were smaller, would the rest of your face look off? If your eyes were a different shape and color, would the top half of your face still fit with your nose and mouth?

You may find that the very features that always bothered you are just right for the rest of your face and, in fact, give you character and your own personal beauty.

You may also find that as you get older, your feelings about your different features may change. You may hate your high forehead right now, but later on, suddenly your forehead will be fine. And you won't quite be able to remember why your natural, perfectly shaped forehead once bothered you so much.

A LITTLE KNOWN FACT

It's hard to believe, but no one is born automatically knowing how to put makeup on or knowing how to buy it. It takes practice. So give yourself a break if it doesn't work out perfectly at first.

COLORS FOR YOU

Before we get into the specifics of makeup, it is important to know your skin tones. From that, you'll know which families of color fit you.

COLOR TEST

Wearing no makeup, take a beige cloth and wrap it around your shoulders, near your face. Then substitute a white cloth. If you look better in the beige color, you probably have a warm-colored complexion with green and yellow undertones; if you looked better in the white cloth, you have cool undertones or blue and red undertones.

Warm skin tones look best in russets, peaches, and browns. Cool skin tones come alive in pinks, mauves, and roses.

With that said, it is good to remember that almost every color has different shades and some of them will have blue undertones and some will have yellow. For example, gray can have yellow or blue undertones, making the gray different colors, suitable for different people. A brown can be rosy-brown or beigey-brown, depending on its undertones.

When choosing makeup colors, follow the tones of your skin, your eyes, and hair. Your clothes change, but not your facial tones.

THE EYES HAVE IT

Eyes are your most mysterious features and also the most fun to make up. Coming in all shapes, sizes, and colors, they reveal your changing moods. Like snowflakes, no two people ever have exactly the same eyes.

Eyeshadow comes in different forms — powder, cream, liquid, and crayon are a few. Powder is best, especially if you have oily skin. It's also easier to use and handle.

There are different ways to apply eyeshadow depending on the look you want. You can go for a single color or experiment with two or more.

If you have cool skin undertones, you'll look best in shades of gray, pink, and pastels. If you have warm skin undertones, then shades of brown, peach, and beige would be best.

Your eyeshadow shouldn't ever completely match your eyes. Contrasting colors are best. For example, if you have blue eyes, try for the correct shades of warm, reddish browns; if you have green eyes, check out plums and grays. If your eyes are brown, camels and warm browns will highlight the gold in your eyes.

The one-color look

Use a neutral color, brushing the color on from the lashes up under the brow. Don't go beyond your brows as you move from the inner eye to the outer portion of the eye.

The two-color look

Brush one color on the eyelid up to the crease and another from the crease up to the brow. If your lids are larger than the area above the crease, then use the darker color on your lids and the lighter color above the crease. If you have smaller lids than the area under the brow, reverse the pattern. The lighter the color, the larger an area will look. Blend the eyeshadow with a cotton swab so it doesn't look like you have on two totally distinct colors. The two-color look works best if both colors are in the same family.

The three-color pattern

For the most dramatic look, use three colors, which will give you the most shading and shaping. You might want to save this look for special occasions. This approach takes the most practice, so don't be discouraged if you can't shade and shape your eyes perfectly the first time you try.

THE EYES HAVE IT

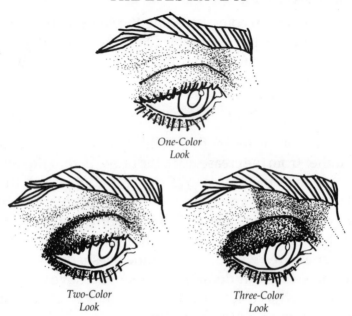

One-Color
Look

Two-Color
Look

Three-Color
Look

Start out with the two-color routine. Take a third color and, starting from the middle of your eyelid along the crease, brush upward and toward your nose. The colors you use on your lid and brow should be less intense in color than the third color. Use a cotton swab to blend these colors so you don't see definite lines of color. The look you want is one that enhances your eyes, not one in which people only notice your makeup.

Or you can add the third, darker color along the line of the crease, blending upward at the outer corner of your eye. Blend!

See what looks best on you and what you're most comfortable with. Do your eyes look better with a lighter color on your lids and a darker color on the underbrow? Or the opposite?

It may be too soon to tell, for your eyes are not completely made up yet.   Remember when it comes to makeup, less is best. You don't want to look like the painted lady, you want to subtly enhance your big, beautiful eyes!

EYELINER

Did you know that Cleopatra had a special slave who put on her eyeliner? Of course she did. How else did she get it on so thick, with the black lines extending way beyond her eyes — you don't think she did that herself!

Eyeliner is very tricky; it can look harsh and unnatural if it isn't put on the correct way. In fact, eyeliner isn't necessary, but if you decide you just gotta have it, choose the crayon type of liner or use your powdered eyeshadow as a liner.

The best look for a liner is a smudged, blended line, accenting the beauty of your eyes. Crayons and eyeshadow can create that look: as with everything else, there are different looks you can create with liner, depending on what you want to do.

✪ The basic look is a thin line of color along the upper lashes and right below the lower lashes, making the line a little thicker as you go toward the outer corner. The bottom line, which is less intense than the top line shouldn't start at the inner corner; it should only cover the outer two-thirds of your eye. The two lines meet at the eye's outer corner. Smudge and blend — of course! Variation:

✪ Place some color very close to the outer corner of the upper and lower lids and smudge it slightly.

✪ It used to be fashionable to put eyeliner (especially pencil and crayon) on the inner edges of your bottom lids. Supposedly, it made your eyes look brighter. Luckily, this is no longer an "in" look, because it's a bad idea. It could be very harmful for your eyes. So, don't do this — it isn't "in" anymore and it could do more damage than it's worth. Instead, line your lower lids *under* the lashes.

THOSE LUSCIOUS LASHES

Thick, black eyelashes — why do the boys always get them? Back in the sixties, the fashion was to draw tiny lines on your upper lids in order to make it look like you had long, thick lashes, or to wear false ones. Yuck! Thank goodness no one does that anymore.

In fact, soft and natural is the "now" look. Don't start wearing mascara everyday. You'll look better without it and it's better for your lashes. Mascara can make your eyelashes brittle, causing them to break and fall out more quickly.

It's fun to wear mascara for special dates, parties and when you're dressing up. So save it for when you want that extra pizzazz!

✪ Stick with water-based mascara, it's better for your eyes. It comes off easier with soap and water and if it gets in your eye, it won't irritate. If you use waterproof mascara, you'll need special makeup remover and you'll probably rub your eyes a lot, causing damage to the skin.

✪ Colors — it's fun to wear blue, green, or gold mascara, but save those colors for special big dates. Choose either black, brown, or the new colorless mascara, whichever looks better. Remember, you want to draw attention to your eyes, not your makeup.

✪ You can put mascara on your top lashes only, on the tips of your top and bottom lashes, or put it completely on your top and bottom lashes. See what looks best to you.

✪ If you put mascara on your lower lashes, hold a tissue under them as you do it, so you don't get makeup on your skin.

✪ Don't cake it on. There's nothing worse than eyes with clumpy mascara.

✪ Eyelash curlers are not necessary. They can hurt your lashes, putting too much pressure on them and causing them to fall out.

GET THOSE EYES IN SHAPE

Sandy has deep-set eyes, which she likes, for her dark lashes contrast with her light green eyes. Madeleine has small eyes, but she loves their rich, mahogany brown. Alice's eyes protrude and yet all she hears is how beautiful they are. Kyle doesn't care that her eyes are set wide apart because everyone tells her how dramatic they are.

These are four girls who supposedly have imperfect eyes, yet there is something special about their eyes that they really like and appreciate.

It's all in how you look at it.

Take a look at your eyes, focus on what you like about them and highlight that. If you still are bothered by the shape or position of your eyes, here are some camouflaging tips.

SHAPE OF EYE	EYESHADOW	EYELINER	MASCARA
Close-set eyes	Brush light shade along upper lid; apply medium-to-dark shadow on outer corners of eyes.	Apply medium-to-dark liner on outer corners of upper and lower lids and smudge.	Put on top, outer lashes only.
Wide-set eyes	Brush medium-to-dark shade on upper lids.	Apply liner on top lids from inner corner of the eye to outer corner; bottom lid line starts closer toward the inner corner. Smudge and blend.	None.
Deep-set eyes	Brush on a shade of shadow along lids that is close to your skin color.	None.	Put mascara on top and bottom lashes.
Prominent eyes	Brush medium-to-dark shade on upper lids, then blend it just above the crease.	None.	Put mascara on top lashes only.
Small eyes	Brush light-to-medium shade along upper lids to outer corner of eyes and along the outer third of lower lids. Blend.	Apply medium-to-dark liner and brush it along outer two-thirds of upper lid.	Put mascara on upper lashes.

THE FINAL TOUCH

Your brows frame your eyes, adding definition.

It's best to leave them alone and let your brows go *au naturel!*

Plucking, waxing, or dyeing them is a terrible idea, and the absolute worst thing to do is to shave your eyebrows. Horrors! Don't touch those brows! They're perfect the way they are.

There! Your eyes are done! Experiment — see what looks best! Rules are definitely made to be broken. Lock yourself in your room and have fun!

THOSE KISSABLE LIPS

Like your signature, your lips are unique to you. Next to your eyes, these beauties attract the most attention. So play them up.

If using colored lip gloss is not for you, try Vaseline. It's a great way to add shine to your lips and protect them at the same time.

But, if you want extra color, you have your choice between lipstick and lip gloss.

We recommend lip gloss. It's usually wetter in look and lighter in color. And the colors range from fun Bubblegum to light Pearl Rose to wild Hot Tamale Red.

Again, if you have warm skin undertones, you can wear russets, peaches, and browns. Cool skin undertones look best in pinks, mauves, and roses. It might be hard to judge yourself in lipstick, so ask a friend.

To make your lips look slightly stained with color, apply the lip gloss, then blot your lips with a tissue until the color doesn't come off on the tissue anymore.

If you want your lips to stand out, use subdued makeup on the rest of your face, using less eye makeup and blush.

If your upper or lower lip is smaller than the other, use a paler color on that lip. If you want your lips to look smaller, use a darker color.

Your lip color shouldn't match your clothes, but neither should the two vie for attention. They should complement each other — Orange Ice lip gloss and a bright red sweater is an absolute don't!

With all the colors out there, such as Georgia Peach, Raspberry Truffle, and Pretty Pink, you can kiss your blues away!

BRUSH ON BLUSH

In *Gone With The Wind*, Scarlett O'Hara pinched her cheeks to make them a bright pink. In the olden days, girls in northern countries used snow to make their cheeks red and glowing.

Luckily, with blush we don't have to pinch our cheeks or wait for winter to get that rosy look. There are different kinds of blush — creams, gels, and powders.

Gels, which are water based, are hard to spread evenly.

Creams, bad for oily skin (a pore clogger), can possibly be good for dry skin, for they are oil based, and they are easy to spread.

Powder is probably your best bet, for it doesn't clog your pores, but it sometimes doesn't look totally natural. The key word as always is BLEND!

If you wear blush and lipstick, they should work together and not clash with each other — keep the shades in the same family. Orange lipstick and pink blush are lethal. If you have warm skin undertones, you'll look best in browns and peaches, if your skin has cool undertones, you'll glow in pinks and roses.

HOW TO APPLY BLUSH

1. Feel your cheekbones.
2. Starting on your bone, under your pupil, place three dots of color, half an inch apart, going back toward your hairline.
3. Blend the color, going back and up along your cheekbones.

   If you have a narrow face, apply most of the blush to the "apples" of your cheeks; if you have a wide face, apply most of the blush closer to your hairline.

   Don't despair — this takes practice. And blend! Avoid circles, lines, and triangles of color.

✪ The purpose of blush is not to let anyone know you're wearing blush. You want a slight, healthy glow of color.

✪ A hint of color along your forehead, down your nose, and on your chin can be attractive. This looks good only if it's really faint — you don't want it to be obvious.

FOUNDATION

"Do I really have to wear it?"

For whatever reason, makeup doesn't stay on your skin easily for very long (which is why throughout history women are always running into powder rooms). Foundation helps makeup stay on smoother and longer. It also makes your skin color even and less blotchy.

Foundation isn't really necessary for young women. It's easy enough to reapply your blush when necessary and you probably don't need to cover up your skin.

It is also very difficult to learn how to put it on without looking like you're dead or wearing a mask, or wearing someone else's skin. You've definitely seen those women who have a line at their jaw, where their foundation ends and their neck begins. Not cool!

It's also difficult to find the right color. If you decide to wear foundation, visit a department store where there are counters of different brands of makeup, and ask for help from someone who wears makeup that you like — whose face you notice, not her makeup. Don't wear any makeup when you go, and test the color along your jaw line. It should match the color of your skin — don't go darker or lighter.

Pick a foundation that matches your skin type. Oil-free for those with really oily skin; water-based for oily and combination skin or those who don't need much coverage; moisturizer-based for those with dry skin. Water-based foundations are the lightest and easiest to put on.

Always apply foundation with a makeup sponge and apply it to clean skin only. Your foundation shouldn't have any fragrance in it.

Ask the saleswoman to show you how to put it on, but first ask if the demonstration is free.

We think that using foundation is not necessary at this age, so why go to the trouble and expense? Ask your mom for her advice. There will be plenty of time to wear foundation when you get older.

REMOVING MAKEUP

Just when you thought it was over, there's one more step — removing your makeup.

Going to bed with your makeup still on and your face unwashed is a sure way to breakout city and possible eye infections.

Buy eye makeup remover, making sure it is without fragrance. Look at the ingredients — make sure it is fine for your skin. You can buy either eye makeup remover pads or just the remover.

Use a ball or wad of cotton (not tissues) and be careful of the fuzz. Shut one eye and gently wipe downward and outward. Using a damp, warm wash-cloth, gently blot away any remaining eye makeup and eye makeup remover.

If you wear lipstick, make sure you've removed all traces of that. You can break out around your mouth. Follow with your regular washing ritual.

YOUR MAKEUP BAG

You might want to keep your makeup together, either for use at home, or if you decide to take it with you when you go out. Depending on what you've decided to wear, here are some basics for your makeup kit.

1. A mirror
2. Lip gloss and/or Vaseline
3. Eyeshadow
4. Blush
5. Mascara
6. Tissues
7. Astringent or moisturizer

MAKEUP CARE AND HINTS

1. Make sure your makeup is water- or glycerin-based and fragrance-free.
2. Don't share your makeup with anyone else.
3. Buy new mascara every two to three months.
4. Put in soft contacts before applying makeup. If you wear hard lenses, see what is more comfortable and safer for you; you don't want cornea abrasions by putting in your lenses and then applying your makeup. Remove contacts before removing makeup.

5. Don't try on makeup on display in stores.
6. Clean your makeup brushes with warm water and shampoo; soak for a few minutes; rinse thoroughly.
7. Don't wear oil-based eye makeup, especially if you wear contacts; it can hurt your eyes.
8. Remember: Less is more.

DESIGNER EYEGLASSES

The days of being called "four-eyes" are over. Today, glasses are definitely a fashion statement. They're so cool that some people wear them even if they don't need them. Your beautiful blues and gorgeous greens won't get lost behind your frames. There are just a few things you need to know to make your eyes look their most alluring. Depending on the shape of your face (see Chapter Seven), certain styles and frames are better.

Your brows should not show above the frames so choose frames that follow your brow line — or as close as possible. If you pick tinted lenses, makeup will look silly behind the color of your glasses.

For those of you who are nearsighted, to compensate for the prescription lenses, follow the guidelines on how to make your eyes look bigger. Farsighted eyes need darker colors of eyeshadow with a touch of liner and mascara.

FACE SHAPE	DO's	DON'Ts
Round Face	Cat's eye-shaped or rectangular frames	Circular frames
Square Face	Rounded or oval frames	Geometric frames
Heart-shaped Face	Frames that are straight across and rounded on the bottom	Cat's eye-shaped frames
Oval Face	Any shaped frames	

☆☆ QUIZ ☆☆

MAKEUP MAGIC — WHO ARE YOU?

1. *When you look in the mirror, you imagine:*
   a. A girl on a Southern plantation.
   b. A girl on the beach, with the wind in her hair.
   c. A girl in a rock band.

2. *Your favorite colors are:*
   a. Soft pastels of all types.
   b. Midnight blue, forest green, sunshine yellow.
   c. Fuchsia pink, lime green, black.

3. *Your closet is filled with:*
   a. Soft, flowing skirts and white, delicate blouses.
   b.Comfortable sweaters, jeans, and boots.
   c.The latest styles.

4. *Your favorite sounds are:*
   a. Violin and harp duets.
   b. Snow scrunching, birds singing, leaves rustling.
   c. Rock 'n' roll, city noises.

5. *You like to:*
   a. Light candles and take a warm bath, reading your favorite novel.
   b. Walk in the woods on beautiful clear day.
   c. See an artsy film and then sit in a cafe and write.

6. *Your perfect adventure would be:*
   a. Going back in time to the court of King Louis XIV with the boy you love.
   b. Sailing, going from island to island in the Pacific Basin.
   c. Visiting cities all around the world, meeting the newest popular artists, musicians, and writers.

7. *If you could be anyone, you would be:*
   a. Jane Eyre, Juliet, Scarlett O'Hara.
   b. Beryl Markham, Amelia Earhart.
   c. Madonna, Cher, Tracy Chapman.

8. *Dancing for you is:*
   a. Ballet, the only true form of dance.
   b. Dancing barefoot on the grass.
   c. Hitting the latest clubs and dancing the night away.

9. *Your favorite foods are:*
   a. Soufflés, strawberries, and chocolate.
   b. Fruits, 24-grain bread, and spring water.
   c. Anything, as long as it's exotic and different.

10. *Your favorite movie would be:*
   a. A love story.
   b. An adventure.
   c. A foreign film.

If you've chosen mostly "a" answers, you are a true romantic. Surround yourself with soft pastel colors, using the most delicate of touches when applying your makeup. When you go out, you might want to add some shimmer to your lipstick and eyeshadow, but nothing too obvious or harsh.

If "b" seemed to be your favorite choice, you're a natural, outdoorsy, casual kind of girl. You might not want to wear much makeup so stick to basics such as mascara and lip gloss. But if you have a hankering for color, experiment with the earth colors for eyeshadow and sometimes get the outdoors look by using blush.

A "c" kind of girl is beyond new wave; she's the next wave. You might want to be more experimental and dramatic with your makeup. You might not want to overdo your makeup for everyday (then again, you might dare it), but for night and those special occasions, add some of those wild colors you love so much and makeup that shines and glitters.

If you have a mix of letters, then obviously you are a girl of different tastes and moods. Follow your heart. You might be new wave for one day, and then need to go romantic to soften all that black clothing. Or rebel by wearing your hiking boots and no makeup, or just the slightest amount of blush to bring the outdoors in. It's all up to you!

COVER GIRLS

After the photographer has put away her cameras, the makeup artist has put away his brushes, and the lights are shut off, how do the models use makeup to feel beautiful?

Surprisingly enough, most of them believe that less is more — just a touch of color is all that's desirable. And they are fanatical about clean skin and protecting their skin from the sun.**

"Use a pale blush that looks like you're blushing."
—Paulina

"You really have to clean your face! If I'm going out, I use mascara, eye pencil — smudged — and a little lipstick...I don't like a lot of color since my lips are big."
—Frederique

"[In the morning, I] just spray my face with spring water, put on light moisturizer... then fly out the door...I have been told to use an SPF#15 sunscreen on my face."
—Rachel Hunter

"I don't wear mascara... eyes softer without. Foundation makes me feel like I'm suffocating... so I wipe it off first chance I get!"
—Jill Goodacre

"To remove makeup, I start with a milk cleanser, spray my face with water, and wipe... then... soap... "
—Cindy Crawford

"I love red lipstick and just a coat of black mascara if I'm going out. It's nice and simple but not everyday-looking."
—Nkemdilim

** *Cosmopolitan,* August 1988, pp. 277-81

From Hair to There

When you look into the mirror, you see this clean, sparkling face, perfectly made up. But something is wrong — something is missing! Or actually, something is taking over your head.

A fright wig, a string mop, a jungle!

Oh no, it's your hair!

It's time to take control and show your hair that you're the boss. This chapter will help you get that hair in shape. Whether it's straight, curly, short, long, limp, or full, correct washing and care are the key elements to beautiful hair.

WASHING YOUR HAIR

There are many similarities between hair and skin. Just as with your skin, your hair and scalp should be treated gently. If you mistreat your hair, it could result in split ends, fly-away, or dull, lifeless hair.

The first step of a good, healthy shampoo is brushing the tangles out of your hair while it's still dry. Your hair should be smooth and tangle-free when you begin your wash. Start from the ends and work up, gently brushing out your hair. Try not to pull your hair at all — indulge your hair and enjoy the feel of the brush easily flowing through your hair. Brush your hair, not your scalp.

✪ Next is the actual shampoo. Your hair and scalp should be thoroughly wet before you apply the shampoo. Warm water is the best temperature for washing. Try not to use extreme hot or cold water on your head. Your hair is the most delicate when it is wet so be careful not to tangle or pull it.

✪ Pour a small amount of shampoo in your palm and then dilute it with water. Don't pour the shampoo directly on your hair. Rub your palms together, spreading the shampoo in your hands. Gently rub your hands through your hair to your scalp, for your scalp produces the oils.

✪ Massage your scalp with your soapy hands, using the pads of your fingers — not your nails. Try not to scratch your scalp or tangle or pull your hair. Massage your entire head, along the hairline. If you are careful, you will find that your hair does not snarl up at all.

✪ One soaping should be enough. Although the instructions on the bottles of shampoo tell you to wash twice, it isn't necessary. Basically, it means you have to buy new shampoo twice as quickly.

✪ Rinse thoroughly, section by section. Lift sections of your hair if you need to get the water to the scalp. Once it feels as if you have gotten all the shampoo out of your hair, rinse again. Rinsing is the main event here.

✪ After you have removed all the shampoo, apply conditioner to your hair — not to your scalp.

✪ Rinse the conditioner out completely.

✪ Do the squeaky clean test. Take a few strands between your fingers and rub gently. If they squeak, you know you've removed the shampoo and conditioner.

✪ Pat or blot your hair dry. Once again be very gentle, for your wet hair is very delicate. If you were careful when you washed your hair, your hair shouldn't be too tangled. If you must comb it, use a wide-tooth comb, starting at the ends and working your way up the hair.

✪ Let it dry naturally if you can. Style your hair while it is still damp.

A WORD ABOUT SHAMPOOS
AND CONDITIONERS

You don't need a conditioner to help remove the snarls from your hair, for if you brush your hair out before you wash it and then shampoo your scalp, gently putting your hands through your hair, your hair won't tangle from washing. Conditioners are like moisturizers. The reason to put it at the ends of your hair is because this hair is the oldest on your head and is the most damaged from brushing, washing, the sun, and whatever else you do.

It is good to alternate between a couple of different shampoos. If you use only one, your hair gets used to it and, after a while, becomes lifeless. If you switch off every other day or every other week, then your hair can't get used to the shampoo.

Shampoos and conditioners each have their own job. Shampoos clean your head and hair. It's best to buy a separate shampoo and conditioner, not one product that has both.

Choose your shampoo, depending on what kind of scalp you have. Choose the conditioner for your hair.

TYPECASTING YOUR HAIR

You can have three different types of hair — curly, wavy, or straight — and three different kinds of textures — fine, coarse, or average.

As with your skin, there are different types of scalps and hair in terms of oiliness and dryness. The best way to tell what kind of scalp you have is to determine what kind of skin you have. It is usually the same. If your skin overproduces oil, the chances are that your scalp will do the same.

CARE FOR YOUR HAIR!

Oily Scalp/Oily Hair
Water-based or oil-free shampoo
Condition ends of hair

Oily Scalp/Dry Hair
Water-based or oil-free shampoo
Condition ends of hair

Dry Scalp/Dry Hair
Creamy shampoo
Condition scalp, weekly deep-conditioning

It's possible to have an oily scalp with oily hair, an oily scalp with dry hair, or a dry scalp with dry hair, which means not enough oil is produced to hold in moisture. You will not find a dry scalp with oily hair.

You can have dry hair even if you have an oily scalp for a number of reasons. It could be that you are over-stimulating your scalp through harsh brushing and washing. You might be overdrying your hair by blow-drying it. Or perhaps you are not washing the shampoo and/or conditioner completely out of your hair and it is causing your hair to look lifeless.

If you don't feel your hair is either extremely dry or oily use a water-based shampoo and condition only the ends of your hair.

BAN YOUR DANDRUFF

According to the ads, dandruff is almost as horrible as pimples and anyone with dandruff should not be let out of the house!

Surprisingly enough though, about ninety percent of adults have dandruff — and they leave their homes and have normal lives.

Some flaking is normal. So if you have very little, please don't worry about it and think you have a major catastrophe on your hands — or shoulders. It's normal. Dandruff occurs for a few different reasons:

1. Sometimes it is as simple as not getting all the shampoo or conditioner out of your hair. Make sure you rinse your head and hair thoroughly.

2. Using the wrong products on your hair, such as a creamy shampoo for an oily scalp, could cause an increase in dandruff.

3. Your scalp may be very dry or very oily. First, try cleaning your scalp or conditioning it if necessary, rinse well, and see what happens. If the condition persists, you might want to use medicated shampoos.

Talk with your mother about buying a medicated shampoo. There might already be one in the house. Don't use it too much or too often because medicated shampoos are strong and can dry out your hair and/or scalp.

When your dandruff starts clearing up, switch back to your regular shampoo and only use the medicated shampoo once a week.

TOOLS OF THE TRADE

What's the point of washing your hair ever-so-carefully if your comb and brush spell danger to it?

The best kind of brush is a natural or boar-bristle brush, for it prevents static electricity and hair breakage. Boar bristle is more expensive than nylon, but nylon-bristled brushes, which are firm and easy to find, are too rough on your hair. On the other hand, ball-tipped synthetic brushes are gentle and less expensive. A good hair brush has a rubber bed.

A wide-tooth comb is the gentlest comb for your hair. It may take a little longer to comb out your hair, but it's worth it to save your hair from breakage.

Wash your tools once a week in soapy water and — you guessed it — rinse thoroughly!

SPORTS-PROOF, WEATHER-PROOF HAIR

Dorothy Hamill perfected the art of having beautiful hair while living the active sports life. Florence Griffith Joyner proved that you can be strong, fast, beautiful, and a winner all at the same time.

Just like these great athletes, your hair can look healthy and terrific while you live the active life all year round.

THE SUMMER SIZZLES

If the summer isn't playing havoc with your skin, it's going after your hair. Between humidity, the sun, and salt water, your hair doesn't have much of a chance, unless you protect it.

You know that humidity can make your fine hair flatter than the proverbial pancake and cause your curly hair to have a life of its own. Suddenly you find yourself starring as "Little Head of Horrors!"

Your hairdryer and hairspray are no match for the summer's humidity — it's time for a mousse attack! With mousse, you can shape your hair into the style you want and it will hold, whether your hair is fine or curly.

If you have curly hair and it frizzes uncontrollably, another option is to go wild and natural. Don't fight it! Find new styles with bandanas, scarfs, and clips and trick your hair into a beautiful shape.

The sun won't burn your hair, but the ultraviolet rays can suck out its moisture, making it brittle and dead-looking. To protect your hair, wear a hat or scarf. Or look for mousse, gel, or other hair products with sunscreen and comb it through your hair. Don't forget to protect your scalp — the sun will burn that.

If the above weren't enough, salt water has to get into the act, too. Salt water leaves your hair tangled, sticky, and dry. If you wet your hair thoroughly with fresh water before you jump in the ocean, your hair will absorb less of the salt water. Or coat your hair with conditioner before you get to the beach and it will protect your hair.

If by some chance you did not protect your hair before beaching, and your hair ends up tangled, dried, and sticky — all is not lost. Don't try to brush it out at the beach, you will break your hair. When you get home, shampoo and condition your hair, and starting from the ends, gently comb it out.

SWIMMING

Chlorine should be outlawed for what it does to your hair. Since it's necessary in swimming pools, you'll have to take precautionary steps to protect your mane.

You can wear a bathing cap. It's usually required, and it protects your hair. Besides, racing caps now come in wild colors. You can even condition your hair and leave the conditioner in, put the swim cap on, swim, and then wash and rinse it out later.

If you don't wear a bathing cap, wet your hair thoroughly with fresh water before entering the pool. The fresh water will prevent your hair from absorbing as much chlorine.

WINTER WEAR & TEAR

Which is worse? Too much moisture or not enough? During the dry winter months, your hair can limp out, sprout wings and fly away, or just look dull.

Once again, mousse can come to your rescue. Stop blow-drying your hair while it's still slightly damp; use a styling mousse or gel, and then let your hair dry naturally. It can give shape and body to dull-looking and staticky hair.

Indoor dry heat robs the moisture from your hair so make sure you condition it regularly. Find a conditioner that has dimethicone or cyclomethicone, which are antistatic ingredients. It will make your hair soft and shiny, and will control fly-away hair.

Definitely use a wide-toothed comb and a natural- or boar-bristle brush; a plastic-bristled brush increases static.

DEAR SMART TALK...

Q. *Is it bad to wash my hair every day?*

A. You can wash your hair every day without damaging it if you use a gentle shampoo. On the days you play sports, save the washing for after your activity so you don't have to wash your hair twice. If, after washing it every day, you see your hair becoming fly-away, it could mean that for you, every day is too often. If that happens, try washing every other day or washing without soap on alternate days.

Q. *A lot of my hair falls out. Am I losing my hair?*

A. It's normal to lose between fifty and eighty strands of hair a day. If more than that is coming out, then get it checked.

Q. *Is it true that brushing your hair one hundred strokes a day is good for it?*

A. It was probably a bald person who made this one up. Overbrushing (and one hundred strokes is definitely overbrushing) can break your hair and make it more oily.

Q. *Some conditioners say you don't have to rinse them out. Is it okay to use them?*

A. It's best to stay away from those conditioners and use the ones that specifically say to rinse thoroughly. The conditioner will attract dirt and could cause excessive oiliness and maybe dandruff.

Q. *How is a clean scalp supposed to feel?*

A. A clean scalp feels smooth, clean, and comfortable, not bumpy, broken out, itchy, or tight.

Q. *Can conditioners cure split ends or make hair fuller?*

A. No. Your hair can look fuller temporarily. Split ends are best handled by getting your hair cut regularly (every three months at least), brushing it gently with the correct brush, washing it gently, not overdrying your hair, and not using too harsh a shampoo.

Q. *Can cutting your hair make it grow faster?*

A. No. It may seem like it, especially if you cut your hair more often in the summer, for your hair grows faster in hot weather.

Hair, Beautiful Hair

*D*o you see your hair as long locks flowing down your back? As a geometric art object? As multi-colored and multi-length?

Your hair says a lot about you — it's another way of expressing yourself and showing who you are.

Now may be the first time that you have a definite say about your hair and what kind of cut and style you want.

Don't panic! This is the fun of growing up. Before going for your new haircut there are some important things to think about:

1. The first thing to decide is how much time you want to spend on your hair. Are you the kind of person who rolls out of bed, shampoos, and goes? Or do you enjoy styling your hair every morning, spending an hour with the blow dryer, mousse, or gel?

2. The next thing to think about is whether you want your haircut to be versatile, or is one basic style fine for you? Do you want both an everyday look and a look for special occasions?

3. Then, think about your lifestyle. Are you very active in sports, dance, or other activities? Is it best for your lifestyle to have an easy-care hairstyle?

4. The last question to think about is how often do you want to cut your hair? The shorter or more layered your cut is, the more frequently you need to get it cut and shaped. Then again, if it is short, you probably don't need to spend a lot of time taking care of it on an everyday basis.

Now, go to the mirror and take a long, hard look at your hair. What do you like best about it? Is it the texture? The color? The length? The wave or curl or the absolute straightness of it?

All right, now you know your hair and what you are willing to do with it. How do you know which hairstyle is best for you?

Start by figuring out the shape of your face.

DRAW YOUR FACE

Once again, go to your trusty mirror — yes, the mirror is your friend — and pull your hair back so it's completely off your face.

FACIAL SHAPES

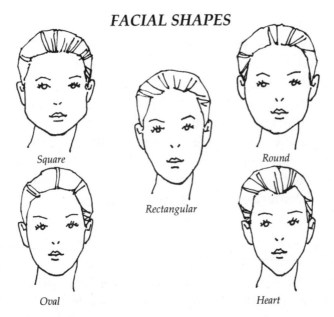

Square

Rectangular

Round

Oval

Heart

Look in the mirror with one eye closed and outline your face in the mirror with a washable crayon or lipstick. Follow your hairline.

1. Is your face almost as wide as it is long?
Your face is round.

2. Is your face wide at the forehead with prominent cheekbones, narrowing down to a small chin?
Your face is triangular or heart-shaped.

3. Is your face evenly proportioned with a wide forehead, high, angular cheekbones and a rounded chin?
Your face is oval.

4. Do you have a wide, square jaw and a wide forehead?
Your face is square.

5. Do you have a long face with a wide, square jaw and a wide forehead?
Your face is rectangular.

SHAPE

If you like your face round, square, oval, heart-shaped, or rectangular, you'll want a cut that emphasizes that look. If you want to play down the angles or the roundness, then you'll go for a cut that almost camouflages the shape of your face.

To make a *round face* look less chubby, create more angles and some length. A center part can lengthen your face if your hair is below your chin. For short hair, an off-center part reduces the roundness.

A *heart-shaped face* needs volume around the chin so the length should be between the chin and mouth, with a side part, which lessens the width of the forehead and cheeks. If your face is more triangular, the best hair length falls to the chin or below.

An *oval face* can take almost any hairstyle. Go for what you like and what looks best.

To soften a *square face*, an off-center part is best. Hair on the forehead softens the angles if the bangs are wispy or off to the side. Hair longer than the chin will lengthen the shape of the face.

Give volume to a *rectangular face* by creating a side part, sweeping the hair across the forehead and fastening it on the side with a barrette. Keeping hair length above the chin is best if you want to decrease the long look. If you have curls, they help soften the angles.

SIZE

If your face is small, you don't want your hair to overwhelm it no matter which shape. Too much volume — and poof — your face will be lost. If you have a large face, a too short or severe style will make your face look even larger.

HAIR TYPE

Also, consider your hair type, which can be curly, wavy, or straight. When you're looking for a hairstyle, pick one that will complement the kind of hair you have. If you have curls, you can get a bouncy, short cut or if your hair is straight, a blunt cut will work well. Take advantage of the kind of hair you have.

GETTING YOUR PERFECT STYLE

Mostly, go for what you like best on you. Enjoy your hair. Don't feel obliged to follow fashion rules.

So now you know the kind of time and energy you want to put into your hair. You know your face shape and what sort of looks will be fine. And you know your hair texture.

Next, hit those magazines and see what hairstyles you like, keeping all the above information in mind. Clip out the photos of the haircuts you like and then see if they fit your lifestyle, your hair, and your own sense of style.

Look around you. Whose hair and haircut do you like? Ask those girls where they got their haircuts and if they are happy with the haircutter. The best way to find a good haircutter is word of mouth.

Get the name of the actual hair stylist, not just the salon, since you want a specific person. Set up a consultation appointment, which will take about ten minutes. It's perfectly reasonable and acceptable to do this. You might want a friend to come with you to give you her opinion, advice, and support. Getting a haircut is an adventure — so have fun!

Bring your pictures and talk with the stylist. He or she might tell you it's not possible to make your hair look like the model's in the magazine, or he or she might agree with your choice. The stylist also may make other suggestions or combine some of the looks in the pictures. Explain what you want from your haircut, but if what you want is a new boyfriend, you're expecting too much from the haircut. Tell the cutter how long you want to spend doing your hair yourself, if you have an intensely busy lifestyle, if you want to use a blow dryer, curling iron, etc. If, at the end of the consultation, you don't like the haircutter's suggestions you can leave and go elsewhere. That's the reason for a consultation first.

If you don't understand what the stylist is saying, ask. If he or she mentions a procedure you've never heard of, ask. There's nothing to be embarrassed about.

If the stylist suggests something you don't want, say so. It is your hair. Don't be talked into anything you don't want.

On a consultation visit, you'll also have the chance to see the salon. Does the style of the place fit you? Does it cater to a young crowd? Find out the salon costs: Is the washing included in the complete cost of the cut? Does conditioning cost extra? Is blow-drying included in the price? You can ask all these questions at the consultation.

You have now decided on your haircutter and you are there for your appointment. Great! If you see that the stylist is cutting your hair differently than you want, speak up. Ask him or her to stop cutting and explain his or her plan.

These are two possible scenarios when your haircut is complete.

1. You're entitled to a second appointment and a recut at no extra charge. Don't be embarrassed — you've paid for a haircut that you should like. You're disappointed because you didn't get what you asked for.

2. You like the cut — hurray! Tip the hairstylist ten to fifteen percent, and if someone washed your hair, tip her or him one or two dollars, depending on the price of the cut.

You can ask the haircutter questions about what kind of shampoo, conditioner, etc. you should use.

Congratulations! You now have a new, beautiful head of hair.

MANE MAGIC

Are you about to scream for help? What are all these mousses, sprays, gels, creams? How do you know what to use, what each one does? Maybe it would be easier to be bald.

Luckily, here's a handy chart.

HAIR HELPERS	WHAT IT DOES	HOW TO USE IT	LOOK
Mousse	Adds volume and lift; builds control; good for limp, thin hair	Use on damp or nearly dry hair; put small amount in hand; rub to dissolve; run through roots and then style; don't use on ends, for it can weigh down hair	Creates finished or tousled look
Gel	Builds wave, body, texture; good for curly or kinky hair	The thicker the gel, the stronger the hold; use on damp hair; create look wanted; let air-dry; then brush out	Creates desired styles and a wet look
Styling Spray	Strong hold, keeps hair in place; can be good for all types of hair	After hair is styled the way you want, spray to keep it in place	Creates a look that will stay
Styling Cream	Gives body, hold, and conditioning; de-frizzes curly and thick hair; good for damaged, dry hair	Using a small amount, put on with fingers	Creates a look that will stay, and a wet look

TRESS TRICKS

Back in the Stone Age, there wasn't much of a choice when it came to different hairstyling tools. Basically, there was the bone, which could be used to curl hair. And there wasn't much the women could do for a last-minute date; they didn't have blow dryers, and there wasn't any privacy at the tribal fire.

Today, there are all sorts of hair tools from which you can choose.

The all-purpose blow dryer is good for spot drying or shaping your hair without the use of rollers. Don't use it on just-out-of-the-shower hair; your hair will be damaged and it won't take shape. Towel-dry to remove excess water. Don't use the hottest temperature, and hold it six to eight inches from your hair. You can buy a diffuser, which forces the hot air into a wider circle, so the harsh heat isn't hitting one, condensed area. You'll probably need to practice if you style your hair with a brush and blow dryer.

CURLS, CURLS, CURLS

Curling irons are great for touch-ups and adding curls. Work in small sections. Curling irons can dry out your hair so use conditioner and don't keep the iron in your hair too long.

Rollers have changed so much over the last twenty years. Luckily, you no longer have to go to bed with big rollers and clips biting into your scalp.

If you choose electric rollers, don't use them at their hottest. Unplug them and wait a few minutes; you don't want to burn your hair. Mist rollers add body to your hair because of the moisture.

There are also the flexible rollers — the kind that bend. You just roll your hair and bend the rods over to keep your hair in place. Your hair can be slightly damp with these rollers or you can set your hair when it's dry and take a shower or a bath, letting the steam do the job for you. These rollers come in great colors and can also be used instead of a barrette or comb to keep your hair up.

Crimpers are somewhat like curling irons, except they crimp rather than curl and make ridges in your hair.

If you want tight curls, use pipe cleaners. Wrap the tip of a small section in the pipe cleaner and roll it toward the scalp. Twist the ends of the pipe cleaner to secure the hair and let it dry; your curls will be as tight or as loose as you roll them.

If you want kinky curls, braid your hair while it's still wet. Let it dry, unbraid and watch your hair transform before your eyes. You can keep it kinky or brush it out a bit with your fingers for a wilder look. It's not a great idea to do this all the time because very tight braids aren't good for your hair. But every once in a while, it's great to have a new look.

COLORING AND PERMING

Do you want some purple streaks to liven up your golden hair? Need more red in your titian tresses?

Dreaming of blonde streaks for your dark brown locks?

Luckily, there are different products that can highlight, color, and sparkle — *and* wash out.

Let's face it — you're too young for permanent hair coloring. Besides, coloring your hair at home can backfire — you want to be able to leave your house and green hair just may not be the look you want.

This is definitely the time to listen to your mother and stick with products that wash out after one or two shampoos.

You can still have fun and experiment with different colors — it's also reassuring that Practically Pumpkin or Boysenberry Blue or Luscious Lime washes out fast and easy.

Or go for highlights, which can add a glow to your hair and still be subtle if you go just a shade or two lighter than your own color. You also don't need to highlight your entire head of hair; you can just focus on the area around your face.

Buy hairspray or mousse with glitter for those nights when you want to sparkle.

Enjoy the hair you have, whether it's straight, curly, or wavy. Everyone wishes their hair were a little different: Straight-haired girls would love some bounce; curly-haired girls want their hair to be straight and dramatic; and wavy-haired girls probably want their hair to be perfectly straight or totally curly. Get a haircut that flatters your face and makes the most of the kind of hair you have.

If, after the most perfect haircut, you still want your straight hair to curl like Shirley Temple's or to have more life to it, there are permanents, which add curl, body, movement, and texture — depending on what you want.

You can get a body wave, which doesn't last as long as a permanent and doesn't create as much of a curl, but adds body to your hair without all the harsh chemicals.

A permanent can give you as much curl as you want, but it's harsher on your hair. You might get more bounce and curl, but you'll get less natural shine. If you choose to get a body wave or a permanent, definitely talk to your parents. And don't do it yourself; let a pro do it, especially one who knows your hair. Body waves and perms are chemical treatments and they can damage your hair. Your best bet is to go *au naturel*!

If you think your hair is ugly and only a perm or a new color will help, wait a while. See if you can add to your hair's natural beauty by styling it differently or getting a new haircut by a new person whose work you've seen. Perms and dyeing are not great for your hair. If you have straight red hair, there is probably someone out there with wavy, brown hair who wishes she had your hair. Give your hair a chance as its natural self.

EXERCISE YOUR RIGHT TO ACCESSORIZE

Throughout the ages, women have added objects to their hair ranging from jewels to feathers to fruit to birds to give it that extra *je ne sais quoi*. You don't have to go as far as birds and fruit, but if you want to spiff up your 'do, bring on the accessories.

Start out by putting your hair up with butterfly clips, plastic-covered rubber bands, or barrettes. Pull your hair back with cloth or plastic headbands, scarves, or combs. Braid bells, buttons, or beads in your hair. Weave ribbons, colorful shoelaces, or beaded necklaces through your hair.

Wrap your ponytail with a satiny, braided coil, which uses velcro to close it. With your basic ponytail, you can twist a bandana in it as you create a bun, with wisps of hair framing your face.

Use a ribbon or scarf and pull your hair back with it, creating a ponytail, use it in place of a headband, or just pull some hair off to the side with it.

If you have short hair, brush your hair to one side of your face and hold your hair in place with a comb or a fun barrette.

Be adventurous and experiment. Transform objects into hair ornaments. Bows and other items for wrapping presents can be great hair ornaments. Dazzle your admirers and use real or silk flowers, and even jewelry to jazz up your hair. Let your imagination go wild and have fun.

WILD STYLES

Short or long, there is always a way to change your hair and look.

LONG & LUXURIOUS HAIRSTYLES

*A Romantic Look with
a Different Twist*

French Braid

Long & Dramatic

LONG AND LUXURIOUS

Straight, curly, or wavy, the options for long hair are endless. Here are just a few ideas:

1. For a classic ponytail with an added twist, pull most of your hair back into a ponytail and anchor it with a coated rubber band. Take the extra section, wrap it around the rubber band and keep it in place with a bobby pin or two.

2. A French braid is still one of the prettiest looks. Comb your hair straight back, off your face. Gather the front section of hair on each side and pull it up and back. Roll one section toward the top of the head, twisting as you roll. Secure it with a comb. Do the same to the other side. Loosely braid the two side sections together with an equal section from the center of the back of the head. Continue braiding, picking up sections of hair from the sides and back/center. Braid hair to the end, tie it with a coated rubberband, tuck under, and pin. *Voilà!* — a French braid.

3. A slightly different look is just as romantic. Brush your hair back and starting at your temples, twist the front sections along your hairline toward the top of your head, adding hair as you move back. Continue until both sides reach the nape of your neck and anchor your hair with a bow.

4. Use long, oblong scarves, and wrap them around your head. If you take two, weave them around each other in front and tie. Pull strands of hair out between the two and let them hang loosely. It will look soft and feminine. Or if you want a more sporty look, use one of your father's old ties.

5. For a more dramatic look, part your hair on one side. On the same side that the part is on, push your hair behind your ear. Let your hair drape across your opposite shoulder and across your forehead.

6. Make a ponytail. Tie a scarf around the rubber band you're using and intertwine the scarf through your hair. If a scarf is too bulky, use brightly colored shoelaces or ribbons.

7. If you have curly or wavy hair, start with it damp. Using mousse, emphasize your curls by scrunching your hair. Using a headband, smooth out the hair on top so that only your loose hair is curly and wild. Pull out some tendrils to soften the look.

SHORT AND SASSY

Here are four easy styles that require just a dab of mousse to help you. Be careful not to weigh down your hair with too much mousse; you can always add if necessary.

SHORT & SASSY HAIRSTYLES

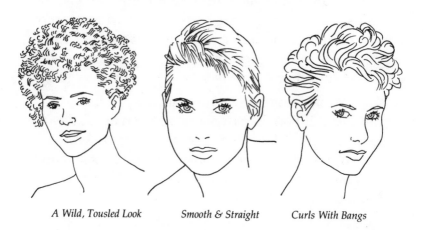

A Wild, Tousled Look   *Smooth & Straight*   *Curls With Bangs*

1. Start with damp hair. Apply mousse to your fingers and just start moving your fingers around your hair in a circular motion, close to your scalp, to create a wild, tousled look.

2. If smooth is more your style, use the mousse to straighten your hair flat back or straight up.

3. Or curl your hair but create straight bangs. You can even shape your bangs, gathering them into a little pointed section on your forehead.

4. Go dramatic with the pageboy look. Towel dry your hair and make a center part. Comb sculpting lotion through to the ends, straightening your hair as you comb. As your bangs air-dry, use your curling iron to turn the ends of your hair under. Do this all the way around your head.

This is just the beginning of all the different styles you have at your fingertips — literally.

Here's Looking at You!

Y ou have it all now! Your skin, your hair, your unique look.

There are just two more beauty secrets you need, which will bring everything together for you.

First, believe in yourself.

Whether you decide to wear makeup or just lip gloss, blow-dry your hair or just shower and go, cut your hair short or let it grow down to your waist, you will look and feel great if you stay true to yourself.

Be proud of yourself and your special look.

Remember how people's skin glows when they're in love? Your skin and hair and all of you will definitely glow when you love yourself and are proud of who you are. It is this inner and outer glow that lights up your beauty.

It really is true that when you feel good about yourself, it shows and radiates through you. In turn, people will feel good about you.

You don't need to be Miss America, a *Seventeen* model, a famous rock star, or the next Nobel Prize winner to feel good about yourself. Being the age you are now, unsure about things, not quite knowing how to wear your hair is all perfectly fine and part of who you are.

Feeling good about yourself is accepting who you are now. This isn't as easy as washing your hair. There are no hard and fast rules for accepting and loving yourself — no diagrams, drawings, or maps.

And it does take time and patience — and practice.

It takes practice to know what you want and know what makes you feel good and true to yourself. You'll be able to tell inside when you are being true to yourself or when you are going along with the crowd when you don't want to.

You've started this journey by taking some of the quizzes that asked you questions about yourself and what you like, before you took anyone else into consideration. Learn what you want and what makes you feel good. Follow your own voice.

Here's the second beauty tip:

Have fun. What's the point of doing any of this if you

don't want to or if it isn't fun for you? Getting a new haircut isn't supposed to be like taking out the garbage; going through magazine pictures isn't supposed to be worse than eating liver; washing your hair isn't supposed to be the same as babysitting your younger brother.

Discovering who you are and what you like is one of the most exciting, challenging, interesting and fun things to do!

What can be more fun than learning about your likes and dislikes? Or experimenting with the kind of makeup you want to wear? Or creating different hairstyles? Or taking care of yourself so you feel and look great?

So, have a blast — being you!